Seumas MacManus, Pamela Colman Smith

In Chimney Corners

Merry Tales of Irish Folklore

Seumas MacManus, Pamela Colman Smith

In Chimney Corners
Merry Tales of Irish Folklore

ISBN/EAN: 9783744733144

Printed in Europe, USA, Canada, Australia, Japan

Cover: Foto ©Thomas Meinert / pixelio.de

More available books at **www.hansebooks.com**

In Chimney Corners.

Merry Tales of Irish Folk Lore

by

Seumas MacManus

Illustrated by
Pamela Colman Smith

New York
Doubleday & McClure Co

To
Our Brave Boys and Girls
who have fared forth from their homes,
travelling away and away, far further than I could
tell you, and twice further than you could
tell me, into the Strange Land Be-
yond, to push their fortune,
THIS BOOK

OUR FOLK-TALES

In those days Ireland had many Kings and Queens, and was populated by good people. It was not bounded by the sea; all around it was a strange country in which, at rare intervals, arose many-windowed castles inhabited by Giants, Kings, Queens, or beautiful Princesses. On occasions, others are acknowledged; as, when the boy from Ireland fought the dragon, or when his marriage with the Princess was celebrated. The mysterious population which turned up at these times was not whilst he had fared forward on his long and lonely journey, with, at most, a single habitation punctuating each day's progress. Whence, then, this population came, and whither it went, I know not; I never knew; for, no further account is taken of it.

Sometimes the young men of Erin sought adventure in their own land, where were both

in plenty. But oftener they went away into
the land of mystery, the Country Beyond.
They were fearless, these boys, and earned the
reward. Some day, long after his kindred had
concluded that he was killed or enchanted, the
adventurer, maybe, emerged again from the
Mysterious Land, with fortune and a beautiful
damsel, and with such tales of wonder as set off
all the other strapping young fellows who had
not yet asked their mother's blessing and gone
forth.

Even down to the days of my childhood the
Country Beyond still was. Every morning I
saw the circle of hills that shut it out. On
many, many, bleak and eerie days, when I,
herding on our hill, crouched and hugged myself in the cosy shelter of a lone thorn, I
watched and watched the rim of those hills, and
was filled with wonder, and with longing for
the day when I should be able to climb them,
and drop into the Land of Adventure. And once
in those days, I remember—and the strange
sensation is still with me—how, having gone a
far journey to the Cormullion uplands after a

strayed wether, I saw the tops of the hills of the Country Beyond.

The day came when I did climb, and climb, to the rim, and look over. And lo! the Land of Mystery had vanished. I can feel the ache at my heart even yet. That the land I sought had been there when I was young and inno-cent, I know. But I had not realised that, year by year, it was melting into the unseen; till with painful suddenness I discovered it was no more.

With us, new folk-tales are being enacted every day. Our Irish boys still rise up and go away to a far land and strange to push their fortune. There are fiery dragons in that land, too, and fell giants, with whom our poor boys struggle sore. There cannot be any princesses there, though; or, the *cailins* at home are better than the princesses abroad; for, when our boys come back with the bags of gold—just as in the stories—they have not damsels also. Jamie Ruadh MacLaughlin of Meenacalliay came back, the pockets of his shop-clothes filled with the gold, and married Rossha MacDiarmuid of the Alt Beag; Myles Griffin of the Haugh, as grand as a king, and every bit as proud, came, and took handsome Grania MacGroarty. I could name a long list of others who did likewise.

In the old folk-tales only our boys went off. But now our poor girls, too, must go. Their mothers cry; and when we are on our knees at night, saying the Rosary, we always pray for the girls and boys who are in the strange land.

Some of them come back again.

Some of them do not find their fortune. They never come. Their mothers in Ireland still cry. The door is open and the hearth bright. If this book happen into the hands of any of these their tears will moisten its merriest page; for, . . . they shall remember . . . They shall remember.

Mary Mother, smooth their rugged road, strengthen their failing hearts, and soften to them the heart of the stranger.

SEUMAS MACMANUS.

CONTENTS

ILLUSTRATIONS

Billy Beg and the Bull

BILLY BEG AND THE BULL

ONCE on a time when pigs was swine, there was a King and a Queen, and they had one son, Billy, and the Queen gave Billy a bull that he was very fond of, and it was just as fond of him. After some time the Queen died, and she put it as her last request on the King that he would never part Billy and the bull, and the King promised that, come what might, come what may, he would not. After the Queen died the King married again, and the new Queen didn't take to Billy Beg, and no more did she like the bull, seeing himself and Billy so *thick*. But she couldn't get the King on no account to part Billy and the bull, so she consulted with a hen-wife what they could do as regards separating Billy and the bull. "What will you give me," says the hen-wife, "and I'll very soon part them?" "Whatever you ask," says the Queen. "Well and good then,"

says the hen-wife, "you are to take to your bed,
making pretend that you are bad with a complaint, and I'll do the rest of it." And, well
and good, to her bed she took, and none of the
doctors could do anything for her, or make out
what was her complaint. So the Queen axed
for the hen-wife to be sent for. And sent for
she was, and when she came in and examined
the Queen, she said there was one thing, and
only one, could cure her. The King asked
what was that, and the hen-wife said it was
three mouthfuls of the blood of Billy Beg's
bull. But the King wouldn't on no account
hear of this, and the next day the Queen was
worse, and the third day she was worse still,
and told the King she was dying, and he'd
have her death on his head. So, sooner nor this,
the King had to consent to Billy Beg's bull being killed. When Billy heard this he got very
down in the heart entirely, and he went doith-
erin' about, and the bull saw him, and asked him
what was wrong with him that he was so
mournful, so Billy told the bull what was
wrong with him, and the bull told him to never
mind, but keep up his heart, the Queen would

never taste a drop of his blood. The next
day then the bull was to be killed, and the
Queen got up and went out to have the delight
of seeing his death. When the bull was led up
to be killed, says he to Billy, "Jump up on my
back till we see what kind of a horseman you
are." Up Billy jumped on his back, and with
that the bull leapt nine mile high, nine
mile deep and nine mile broad, and came
down with Billy sticking between his
horns. Hundreds were looking on dazed at
the sight, and through them the bull rushed,
and over the top of the Queen, killing her dead,
and away he galloped where you wouldn't
know day by night, or night by day, over high
hills, low hills, sheep-walks, and bullock-traces,
the Cove of Cork, and old Tom Fox with his
bugle horn. When at last they stopped, "now
then," says the bull to Billy, "you and I
must undergo great scenery, Billy. Put your
hand," says the bull, " in my left ear, and you'll
get a napkin, that, when you spread it out, will
be covered with eating and drinking of all
sorts, fit for the King himself." Billy did this,
and then he spread out the napkin, and ate and

drank to his heart's content, and he rolled up the napkin and put it back in the bull's ear again. "Then," says the bull, "now put your hand into my right ear and you'll find a bit of a stick; if you wind it over your head three times, it will be turned into a sword and give you the strength of a thousand men besides your own, and when you have no more need of it as a sword, it will change back into a stick again." Billy did all this. Then says the bull, "At twelve o'clock the morrow I'll have to meet and fight a great bull." Billy then got up again on the bull's back, and the bull started off and away where you wouldn't know day by night, or night by day, over high hills, low hills, sheep-walks and bullock-traces, the Cove of Cork, and old Tom Fox with his bugle horn. There he met the other bull, and both of them fought, and the like of their fight was never seen before or since. They knocked the soft ground into hard, and the hard into soft, the soft into spring wells, the spring wells into rocks, and the rocks into high hills. They fought long, and Billy Beg's bull killed the other, and drank his blood. Then Billy took the napkin out of his ear again

and spread it out and ate a hearty good dinner.
Then says the bull to Billy, says he, "at twelve
o'clock to-morrow, I'm to meet the bull's
brother that I killed the day, and we'll
have a hard fight." Billy got on the
bull's back again, and the bull started
off and away where you wouldn't know
day by night, or night by day, over high hills,
low hills, sheep-walks and bullock-traces, the
Cove of Cork, and old Tom Fox with his bugle
horn.   There he met the bull's brother that he
killed the day before, and they set to, and they
fought, and the like of the fight was never seen
before or since. They knocked the soft ground
into hard, the hard into soft, the soft into
spring wells, the spring wells into rocks, and
the rocks into high hills.   They fought long,
and at last Billy's bull killed the other and
drank his blood. And then Billy took out the napkin out of the bull's ear again and spread it out
and ate another hearty dinner. Then says the
bull to Billy, says he—"The morrow at twelve
o'clock I'm to fight the brother to the two bulls
I killed—he's a mighty great bull entirely, the
strongest of them all; he's called the

Black Bull of the Forest, and he'll be
too able for me.   When I'm dead," says
the bull, "you, Billy, will take with you
the napkin, and you'll never be hungry; and the stick, and you'll be able to overcome everything that comes in your way; and
take out your knife and cut a strip of the hide
off my back and another strip off my belly
and make a belt of them, and as long as you
wear them you cannot be killed."   Billy was
very sorry to hear this, but he got up on the
bull's back again, and they started off and away
where you wouldn't know day by night or
night by day, over high hills, low hills, sheep-
walks and bullock-traces, the Cove of Cork and
old Tom Fox with his bugle horn.   And sure
enough at twelve o'clock the next day they met
the great Black Bull of the Forest, and both of
the bulls to it, and commenced to fight, and the
like of the fight was never seen before or since;
they knocked the soft ground into hard ground,
and the hard ground into soft and the soft into
spring wells, the spring wells into rocks, and
the rocks into high hills. And they fought long,
but at length the Black Bull of the Forest killed

Billy Beg's bull, and drank his blood. Billy Beg was so vexed at this that for two days he sat over the bull neither eating or drinking, but crying salt tears all the time. Then he got up, and he spread out the napkin, and ate a hearty dinner for he was very hungry with his long fast; and after that he cut a strip of the hide off the bull's back, and another off the belly, and made a belt for himself, and taking it and the bit of stick, and the napkin, he set out to push his fortune, and he travelled for three days and three nights till at last he come to a great gentleman's place. Billy asked the gentleman if he could give him employment, and the gentleman said he wanted just such a boy as him for herding cattle. Billy asked what cattle would he have to herd, and what wages would he get. The gentleman said he had three goats, three cows, three horses and three asses that he fed in an orchard, but that no boy who went with them ever came back alive, for there were three giants, brothers, that came to milk the cows and the goats every day, and killed the boy that was herding; so if Billy liked to try, they wouldn't fix the wages till they'd see if he

would come back alive. "Agreed, then," said
Billy. So the next morning he got up and
drove out the three goats, the three cows, the
three horses, and the three asses to the orchard
and commenced to feed them. About the middle of the day Billy heard three terrible roars
that shook the apples off the bushes, shook the
horns on the cows, and made the hair stand
up on Billy's head, and in comes a frightful big
giant with three heads, and begun to threaten
Billy. "You're too big," says the giant, "for
one bite, and too small for two. What will I
do with you?" "I'll fight you," says Billy, says
he stepping out to him and swinging the bit of
stick three times over his head, when it changed
into a sword and gave him the strength of a
thousand men besides his own. The giant
laughed at the size of him, and says he, "Well,
how will I kill you? Will it be by a swing by
the back,* a cut of the sword, or a square round
of boxing?" "With a swing by the back," says
Billy, "if you can." So they both laid holds,
and Billy lifted the giant clean off the ground,
and fetching him down again sunk him in the

*A wrestle.

earth up to his arm-pits. "Oh, have mercy,"
says the giant. But Billy, taking his sword,
killed the giant, and cut out his tongues. It was
evening by this time, so Billy drove home the
three goats, three cows, three horses, and three
asses, and all the vessels in the house wasn't
able to hold all the milk the cows give that
night.

"Well," says the gentleman, "This beats me,
for I never saw anyone coming back alive out
of there before, nor the cows with a drop of
milk. Did you see anything in the orchard?"
says he. "Nothing worse nor myself," says
Billy. "What about my wages, now," says
Billy. "Well," says the gentleman, "you'll
hardly come alive out of the orchard the morrow. So we'll wait till after that." Next
morning his master told Billy that something
must have happened one of the giants, for he
used to hear the cries of three every night, but
last night he only heard two crying. "I don't
know," says Billy, "anything about them."
That morning after he got his breakfast Billy
drove the three goats, three cows, three horses,
and three asses into the orchard again, and be-

gan to feed them. About twelve o'clock he heard three terrible roars that shook the apples off the bushes, the horns on the cows, and made the hair stand up on Billy's head, and in comes a frightful big giant, with six heads, and he told Billy he had killed his brother yesterday, but he would make him pay for it the day. "Ye're too big," says he, "for one bite, and too small for two, and what will I do with you?" "I'll fight you," says Billy, swinging his stick three times over his head, and turning it into a sword, and giving him the strength of a thousand men besides his own. The giant laughed at him, and says he, "How will I kill you— with a swing by the back, a cut of the sword, or a square round of boxing?" "With a swing by the back," says Billy, "if you can." So the both of them laid holds, and Billy lifted the giant clean off the ground, and fetching him down again, sunk him in it up to the arm-pits. "Oh, spare my life!" says the giant. But Billy taking up his sword, killed him and cut out his tongues. It was evening by this time, and Billy drove home his three goats, three cows, three horses, and three asses, and what milk the cows

gave that night overflowed all the vessels in the house, and, running out, turned a rusty mill that hadn't been turned before for thirty years. If the master was surprised seeing Billy coming back the night before, he was ten times more surprised now.

"Did you see anything in the orchard the day!" says the gentleman. "Nothing worse nor myself," says Billy. "What about my wages now," says Billy. "Well, never mind about your wages," says the gentleman till the morrow, for I think you'll hardly come back alive again," says he. Well and good, Billy went to his bed, and the gentleman went to his bed, and when the gentleman rose in the morning says he to Billy, "I don't know what's wrong with two of the giants; I only heard one crying last night." "I don't know," says Billy, "they must be sick or something." Well, when Billy got his breakfast that day again, he set out to the orchard, driving before him the three goats, three cows, three horses and three asses and sure enough about the middle of the day he hears three terrible roars again, and in comes

another giant, this one with twelve heads on
him, and if the other two were frightful, surely
this one was ten times more so. "You villain,
you," says he to Billy, "you killed my two
brothers, and I'll have my revenge on you now.
Prepare till I kill you," says he; "you're too
big for one bite, and too small for two; what
will I do with you?" "I'll fight you," says Billy,
shaping out and winding the bit of stick three
times over his head. The giant laughed heartily
at the size of him, and says he, "What way do
you prefer being killed? Is it with a swing by
the back, a cut of the sword, or a square round
of boxing?" "A swing by the back," says
Billy. So both of them again laid holds, and
my brave Billy lifts the giant clean off the
ground, and fetching him down again, sunk
him down to his arm-pits in it. "Oh, have
mercy; spare my life," says the giant. But
Billy took his sword, and, killing him, cut out
his tongues. That evening he drove home his
three goats, three cows, three horses, and three
asses, and the milk of the cows had to be turned
into a valley where it made a lough three miles

long, three miles broad, and three miles deep, and that lough has been filled with salmon and white trout ever since. The gentleman wondered now more than ever to see Billy back the third day alive. "Did you see nothing in the orchard the day, Billy?" says he. "No, nothing worse nor myself," says Billy. "Well that beats me," says the gentleman. "What about my wages now?" says Billy. "Well, you're a good mindful boy, that I couldn't easy do without," says the gentleman, "and I'll give you any wages you ask for the future." The next morning, says the gentleman to Billy, "I heard none of the giants crying last night, however it comes. I don't know what has happened to them?" "I don't know," says Billy, "they must be sick or something." "Now, Billy," says the gentleman, "you must look after the cattle the day again. while I go to see the fight." "What fight?" says Billy. "Why," says the gentleman, "it's the king's daughter is going to be devoured by a fiery dragon, if the greatest fighter in the land, that they have been feeding specially for the last three months, isn't able to kill the dragon first. And if he's able to kill the dragon the king is to give him the daughter in marriage." "That will be fine," says Billy. Billy drove out his three goats, three cows, three horses, and three asses to the orchard that day again, and the like of all that passed that day to see the fight with the man and the fiery dragon, Billy never witnessed before. They went in coaches and carriages, on horses and jackasses, riding and walking, crawling and creeping. "My tight little fellow," says a man that was passing to Billy, "why don't you come to see the great fight?" "What would take the likes of me there?" says Billy. But when Billy found them all gone he saddled and bridled the best black horse his master had, and put on the best suit of clothes he could get in his master's house, and rode off to the fight after the rest. When Billy went there he saw the king's daughter with the whole court about her on a platform before the castle, and he thought he never saw anything half as beautiful, and the great warrior that was to fight the dragon was walking up and down on the lawn before her, with three men carrying his sword, and every one in the whole country gathered there looking at him. But when the fiery dragon came up with twelve heads on him, and every mouth of him spitting fire, and let twelve roars out of him, the warrior ran away and hid himself up to the neck in a well of water, and all they could do they couldn't get him to come and face the dragon. Then the king's daughter asked if there was no one there to save her from the dragon, and get her in marriage. But not one stirred. When Billy saw this, he tied the belt of the bull's hide round him, swung his stick over his head, and went in, and after a terrible fight entirely, killed the dragon. Every one then gathered about to find who the stranger was. Billy jumped on his horse and darted away sooner than let them know; but just as he was getting away the king's daughter pulled the shoe off his foot. When the dragon was killed the warrior that had hid in the well of water came out, and

cutting the heads off the dragon he brought
them to the king, and said that it was he who
killed the dragon, in disguise; and he claimed
the king's daughter. But she tried the shoe on
him and found it didn't fit him; so she said it
wasn't him, and that she would marry no one
only the man the shoe fitted. When Billy got
home he changed the clothes again, and had the
horse in the stable, and the cattle all in before
his master came. When the master came, he
began telling Billy about the wonderful day
they had entirely, and about the warrior hiding
in the well of water, and about the grand
stranger that came down out of the sky in a
cloud on a black horse, and killed the fiery
dragon, and then vanished in a cloud again.
"And, now," says he, "Billy, wasn't that wonderful?" "It was, indeed," says Billy, "very
wonderful entirely." After that it was given
out over the country that all the people were to
come to the king's castle on a certain day, till
the king's daughter would try the shoe on them,
and whoever it fitted she was to marry them.
When the day arrived Billy was in the orchard

with the three goats, three cows, three horses,
and three asses, as usual, and the like of all the
crowds that passed that day going to the king's
castle to get the shoe tried on, he never saw before. They went in coaches and carriages, on
horses and jackasses, riding and walking, and
crawling and creeping. They all asked Billy
was not he going to the king's castle, but Billy
said, "Arrah, what would be bringin' the likes
of me there?" At last when all the others
had gone there passed an old man with a very
scarecrow suit of rags on him, and Billy
stopped him and asked him what boot would he
take and swap clothes with him. "Just take
care of yourself, now," says the old man, "and
don't be playing off your jokes on my clothes,
or maybe I'd make you feel the weight of this
stick." But Billy soon let him see it was in
earnest he was, and both of them swapped
suits, Billy giving the old man boot. Then off
to the castle started Billy, with the suit of rags
on his back and an old stick in his hand, and
when he come there he found all in great commotion trying on the shoe, and some of them

cutting down their foot, trying to get it to fit. But it was all of no use, the shoe could be got to fit none of them at all, and the king's daughter was going to give up in despair when the wee ragged looking boy, which was Billy, elbowed his way through them, and says he, "Let me try it on; maybe it would fit me." But the people when they saw him, all began to laugh at the sight of him, and "Go along out of that, you example you," says they shoving and pushing him back. But the king's daughter saw him, and called on them by all manner of means to let him come up and try on the shoe. So Billy went up, and all the people looked on, breaking their hearts laughing at the conceit of it. But what would you have of it, but to the dumfounding of them all, the shoe fitted Billy as nice as if it was made on his foot for a last. So the king's daughter claimed Billy as her husband. He then confessed that it was he that killed the fiery dragon; and when the king had him dressed up in a silk and satin suit, with plenty of gold and silver ornaments everyone gave in that his like they never saw afore. He

was then married to the king's daughter, and
the wedding lasted nine days, nine hours, nine
minutes, nine half minutes and nine quarter
minutes, and they lived happy and well from
that day to this. I got brogues of *brochan**
and breeches of glass, a bit of pie for telling a
lie, and then I came slithering home.

---

* Porridge.

Murroghoo-More and Murroghoo-Beg

MURROGHOO-MORE AND
MURROGHOO-BEG

MURROGHOO-MORE and Murroghoo-beg were cousins and lived in the one townland. Murroghoo-more was the biggest and strongest and always kept poor Murroghoo-beg at his command, and made him do what he liked. Murroghoo-more one day gave Murroghoo-beg a skillet and says he to him, "Murroghoo-beg, go out to the wood and pluck the full of that skillet of raspberries." Murroghoo-beg took the skillet and went to the wood and filled it with the raspberries, but on the way home again there come on a shower, and Murroghoo-beg had to go in under a bush till it would pass over. When he was in under the bush he began to take the hunger, and when he looked at the fine skillet of ripe raspberries he was carrying home to lazy Murroghoo-more his teeth began to water, and poor Murroghoo-beg couldn't help tasting one raspberry just to see what they were like, and then another, and another, till at last he finished the skillet. Very well and good. When he came home, says Murroghoo-more, "Where's the raspberries I sent ye for?" "I had the full of the skillet, but hunger took me on the road home, and I ate them," says Murroghoo-beg. So Murroghoo-more thrashed him soundly. Well the next morning Murroghoo-more come to Murroghoo-beg again, and gave him the skillet, and told him to go to the wood and pull him a skillet of raspberries; "and mind," says he, "that hunger doesn't take you on the way home the day, or it will be worse for ye." Poor Murroghoo-beg promised that it would not, and he set out this day again and pulled the full of the skillet of raspberries in the wood; and on his way home doesn't a shower come on again and put him under a bush, and the hunger took him again, and he ate the skillet of raspberries. So when he went home Murroghoo-more asked him where was his raspberries, and poor Murroghoo-beg told him again what happened to him. "All right," says Murroghoo-more, and he set to and thrashed

Murroghoo-beg soundly. Very good, the next morning Murroghoo-more comes to Murroghoo-beg the third time, and gave him the skillet and told him to go out to the wood and pull him a skillet of raspberries, and that if he ate the raspberries this time again he would surely have his life. But poor Murroghoo-beg ate a hearty breakfast, and said there was no fear of the hunger taking him the day. So out he goes to the wood and fills his skillet again, and set out whistling to carry it home to Murroghoo-more. But what would you have of it but the shower put Murroghoo-beg anunder the bush, and the hunger took him and he ate the skillet of raspberries again. Then he went home to Murroghoo-more, and says Murroghoo-more, "Where's my skillet of raspberries I sent you to the wood to pluck for me." "Och!" says Murroghoo-beg, says he, "the hunger took me and I ate them." "All right," says Murroghoo-more, "ye must die. I'll pick out your eyes first, and then I'll leave it to yourself to choose how to die after." So he got a pointed stick, and setting it on fire, he put it into poor Murro-

ghoo-beg's eyes and burned them out. "Now,"
says Murroghoo-more, "what am I to do with
you?" "Well," says Murroghoo-beg, says he,
"I suppose the easiest death will be to leave me
over in that old church all night, for no one
that stops a night there is ever alive in the
morning." Very well and good. Murroghoo-
more took poor Murroghoo-beg over to the old
church and left him there. About midnight
poor Murroghoo-beg hears the roolie-boolie
and helter-skelter, and in comes a whole rajimint of cats. Murroghoo-beg got under some
planks in the corner, so he wasn't seen, but
could hear all the cats would say. After a lot of
chat they proposed to tell stories. So they
squared themselves round, and then they dif-
fered on which of them would tell the first
story. Every one of them put it to an older
one till at length it came to an old granny cat,
and she consented to tell her story, but she said
the house would have to be well searched first,
for it wouldn't do for anyone to overhear what
she had to say. Well and good, all the young
cats went hurry skurry round the church, looking under the seats and everywhere, and poor

Murroghoo-beg begun to tremble in his skin
now with fear of being caught, for he knew
they would tear him to pieces. But the young
cats were in such a hurry to hear the old granny
cat's story that they forgot to look under the
planks where Murroghoo-beg was hid. Then
they reported there was no one in the house nor
round about it, so the old cat begun her story.

"Well," says she, "the daughter of the king
is lying bad, and very bad, and she has been
that way now, off and on, for twelve months,
only it's what it's worse she is getting every
day, and all the first doctors in the land have
been called in, and the king has offered her
weight in gold to the man that will cure her,
but it's all of no use. None of them can make
out what's wrong with her, or how she can be
cured. But I know her complaint and know
how to cure it, and I'll tell you it all, only you
must promise never to come out with it, for I
mean to let her die a lingering death," says she.

They all promised that they'd never split lips
again on the subject, so the spiteful old cat
went on—

"Well, then," says she, "long ago, when she

was a child, she saw me putting my head into a
noggin of sweet-milk, and she came up and
hit me on the head, and made me drop the
mouthful I had got, back into the pail again,
and she then took a drink out of the pail herself
with the venom of my spittal in it, and from
that day young serpents have been growing in
her. There's one thing, and only one, would
cure her, and rid her of the serpents, and that,
please the devil, she'll never have, nor never
know of—that is, just three spoonfuls of
water out of the well here at the back of the
church, to be taken nine mornings on the bare
stomach, fasting."

Murroghoo-beg heard all this, and he waited
till the cats went all away, and in the morning
he came out, and, groping his way to the well,
he took off his boots and filled one of them with
water, and then started for the king's palace,
and when he come there all that place was in a
commotion with all the first doctors of the three
kingdoms and France besides. And when poor
Murroghoo-beg come in, and he was asked
what was wrong with him, and he said he had
come to cure the king's daughter; and they

asked him where was his medicine, and he said
he had it in his boot, they commenced laughing
at him, and the doctors ordered him to be
turned out.   And the servants begun to shove
and push poor Murroghoo-beg to put him out
of the palace, but Murroghoo wasn't for going,
and that was the roolie-boolie!   And by the
toss o' wars what with the wrestling and the
fighting and the racketing they made, doesn't
the sick lady hear it, and she sent down word to
know what was going on.   And they sent back
the word that it was a poor demented man that
wanted to cure her ladyship with a bootful of
spring water.   "Let him come up," said her
ladyship; "sure he can't do no worse nor
the rest of them anyhow."   Well, her wish,
of course, was a command.   Up my brave Murroghoo-beg was taken, and when he come
into her ladyship's presence he told her he
would get her out of bed in short time.   So
he put her under cure of three spoonfuls of the
water he had in his boot, on the bare stomach
fasting for nine mornings.   The other doctors
looked on and shook their heads, but daren't
say anything.   But the tables were soon turned

on them, for sure enough the very first day she
took the water she felt great ease entirely, and
so on day after day, till on the morning of the
ninth day after she had took the medicine she
was taken with a fit of vomiting, and vomited
up the full of a basin of young serpents, and
then she got up out of her bed, and walked out
as fine, strong, and handsome a young woman
as you would ask to see.   And she was so well
pleased at this, and the king was so well pleased
that they sent home Murroghoo-beg with double her weight in gold along with him.   After
Murrobhoo-beg came home he went to the well
behind the old church for nine mornings bath-
ing his eyes in it every morning, and on the
ninth morning his eyes and his eyesight were as
good as ever.   Poor Murroghoo-beg could now
live happy and well for the remainder of his
days, only the dread was in him still of Murroghoo-more, and he knew that when Murroghoo-more would hear of his good luck he
would put him to death, and take his gold. And
right enough it wasn't long till it come to Murroghoo-more's ears that Murroghoo-beg was
back alive again with his eyes and eyesight, and

no end of gold into the bargain, however he
had come by it. So my brave Murroghoo-more
starts out and comes to Murroghoo-beg, and,
"Murroghoo-beg," says he, "I thought I left ye
for death; and is it here ye are now?" "Oh,"
says Murroghoo-beg, "but it was you that did
me the good turn entirely. Here I am now
with eyes and my eyesight, and a good bag of
gold into the bargain; and if you would only
put out my eyes and leave me overnight in the
old church again, I think I would have still better luck this time." "How is that?" says Murroghoo-more. "Why," says Murroghoo-beg,
this is the way of it"—and he commences telling Murroghoo-more about how there was a
lot of cats came every night to the old church,
and commenced to tell stories every one of them
about where there was no end of treasure hid,
and about wonderful easy cures for eyes that
would be picked out of men's heads, till he had
Murroghoo-more beside himself with delight.
"You must take and pick out my eyes, now,"
says Murroghoo-more, "and leave me in the old
church the night." "Very good," says Murroghoo-beg, "I'll do that with a heart and a

half." So reddening a pointed stick in the fire Murroghoo-beg picked out the eyes of Murroghoo-more, and took him to the old church, and hid him under the same planks he had been under himself. And there Murroghoo-more lay till midnight, when he hears the roolie-boolie starting, and in comes tumbling the cats. "Och, square round, square round," the young ones begun to cry till we tell stories. "Now," says Murroghoo-more to himself, "now I'm in for it." "I'll tell no more stories," says the old granny cat, "for the last night that I told the story about the king's daughter you didn't search the house rightly, and Murroghoo-beg was lying hid there under them planks in the corner, and he heard the whole rehearsal and went off and cured her—bad luck to him and her!—and got double her weight in gold for it, and cured his own eyes that had been picked out by Murroghoo-more into the bargain." "Oh, but," says the young cats, "we'll search better this night, and I'll warrant you we'll look under the planks, and may the Lord pity Murroghoo-beg if he's eavesdropping again." So off they set at

a gallop to search the house, beginning
first by looking under the planks; and
when they went in there, oh, that was the ruction and the uproar, and out they comes, haul-
ing Murroghoo-more with them, and when the
old cats saw this they come bouncing down,
spitting, and their eyes flashing fire, and all of
them fell on him, tearing him to pieces, and it
was trying to see who would get most of
him they were. So, when Murroghoo-beg
went to the old church in the morning to see
what had become of Murroghoo-more, he got
nothing only a rickle of bare bones. Murroghoo-beg buried these, and went home and
lived happy ever after.

The Queen of the Golden Mines

THE QUEEN OF THE GOLDEN MINES

ONCE on a time there was a King of Ireland, and he had three sons, Teddy, Billy, and Jack. Teddy and Billy was the two eldest, and they were brave able boys. But Jack was the youngest, a *gauchy, dawnic* sort of a lad that was good for nothing only feeding fowls and doing odd turns about the house. When they grew up to be men, Teddy and Billy one day said they'd go away to travel and see the world, for they'd only be good-for-nothing omadhauns if they'd stay here all their lives. Their father said that was good, and so off the both of them started. And that night when they halted from their travelling, who does they see coming up after them, but Jack; for it seems he commenced to think *long,* when he found them gone, and he was that lonesome that he couldn't stay behind them. And there he was dressed in his old tat-

37

tered clothes, a spec-*tacle* for the world, and a
disgrace to them; for of course, they were done
off with the best of everything—rale gentlemen,
as becomed their father's sons. They said to
themselves they'd be long sorry to let that picthur with them—for he *was* a picthur, and no
doubt of it—to be an upcast to them wherever
they'd go. So before they started on again next
mornin' they tied Jack to a millstone, and left
him there. That night again, when they went
to stop from their travellin', what would you
have of it but there was me brave Jack once
more, not a hundred parches behind them, and
he dragging the millstone after him. Teddy
and Billy said this was too bad entirely; and
next day, before they started again, they tied
another millstone to him, and they said, "Well,
you'll not get away from here in a hurry anyhow, boy." So on they went again on their
journey, laughing and cracking jokes, and telling passages, to pass the time; but that night
again, when they went to stop from their journey, lo! and behold ye, who does they see coming tearing after them but my poor Jack, once
more, with the two millstones dragging behind

him. Then they were in a quandhary entirely,
and they begun to consider what was best to
do with him, for they saw there was no holdin'
or tyin' of him, or keepin' him back at all, at all,
for if they were to tie him to a mountain in the
mornin', he'd be afther them with the mountain
rattling at his heels again' night. So they come
to the conclusion that it was best to take Jack
with them, and purtend him to be their hired
boy, and not their brother at all. Of course,
me poor Jack, that was always agreeable, was
only too ready to go on these terms; and on the
three of them went, afore them, till at length
they reached the King of England's castle.
When the King of England heard Teddy and
Billy was the King of Ireland's two sons, he
give them *ceud mile failte,* was plaised and
proud to see them, ordhered them to be made
much of, then opened his hall door, an' asked in
the nobility an' genthry of the whole counthry
side to a big dinner and ball that he gave in
their honour. But what do you have of it, but
in the middle of the ball doesn't Teddy have a
fall out with the King of England's son, and
sthruck him, and then that was the play! The

hubbub and *hooroosh* got up, and the King
ordhered the ball to be stopped, and had Teddy
taken pres'ner, and Billy and Jack ordhered
away out of the kingdom. Billy and Jack went
away, vexed in their hearts at leaving Teddy
in jail, and they travelled away till they came to
France, and the King of France's Castle. Here
when the King of France heard that Billy, the
King of Ireland's son, had come to see him he
went out and welcomed him, an' asked in himself and Jack to come in and make a visit with
him. And, like the King of England, he
thought he couldn't make too much of the King
of Ireland's sons, and threw open his hall door
and asked in the whole nobility and clergy and
genthry of all the country side into a great dinner and ball given in Billy's honour. But lo!
and behould ye, doesn't it turn up at this ball,
too, that Billy had a squabble with the King of
France's son and struck him, and the ball was
stopped by the King's ordhers, and the people
sent home, and Billy taken prisoner, and there
was poor Jack now left all alone. The King of
France, taking pity on Jack, employed him as
a boy. And Jack was getting along very well

at Court, and the king and him used to have
very great yarns together entirely. At length
a great war broke out betwixt France and
Germany; and the King of France was in great
trouble, for the Germans were slaughtering
and conquering all before them. Says Jack,
says, he to the King one day, "I wish I had only
half a rajimint of your men, and you'd see
what I would do." Instead of this the King
gave him a whole army, and in less nor three
days there wasn't a German alive in the whole
kingdom of France. It was the king was the
thankful man to Jack for this good action, and
said he never could forget it to him. After that
Jack got into great favour at Court, and used
to have long chats with the Queen herself. But
Jack soon found that he never could come into
the Queen's presence that he didn't put her in
tears. He asked her one day what was the mean-
ing of this, and she told him that it was because she never looked on him that he didn't put
her in mind of her infant son that had, twelve
months' before, been carried away by the Queen
of the Golden Mines, and who she had never
heard tale or tidings of from that day to this.

"Well, be this and be that," says Jack, says he, "but I'm not the man to leave ye in your trouble if I can help it; and be this and be that over again," says he, "but I won't sleep two nights in the one bed, or eat two meals' meat in the one house, till I find out the Queen of the Golden Mines's Castle, and fetch back your infant son to ye—or else I'll not come back livin,." "Ah," says the Queen, "that would never do!" and "Ah," says the King, "that would never do at all, at all!" They pointed out and showed to him how a hundred great knights had gone on the same errand before him, and not one of them ever come back livin', and there was no use in him throwin' away his life, for they couldn't afford to lose him. But it was all no use; Jack was bound on goin', and go he would. So, the very next morning he was up at cock-crow, and afther leavin' good-bye with the whole of them, and leavin' the King and the Queen in tears, he started on his journey. And he travelled away afore him, inquiring his way to the Castle of the Queen of the Golden Mines; and he travelled and tramped for many a weary day, and for many a weary week, and for many

a weary month; till at last when it was drawing on twelve months from the day he left the Castle of the King of France, one day tors't evening he was travelling through a thick wood, when he fell in with an old man, resting, with a great bundle of sticks by his side; and "Me poor old man," says Jack, says he, "that's a mighty great load entirely for a poor man of your years to be carryin'. Sure, if ye'll allow me, I'll just take them with me, for ye, as far as you're goin'." "Blissins on ye!" says the ould man; "an' an ould man's blissin' atop of that; an' thanky." "Nobbut, thanky, yerself, for your good wishes," says Jack, says he, throwin' the bundle of sticks on his shoulder, an' marchin' on by the ould man's side. And they thravelled away through the wood till they come at last to the ould man's cabin. And the ould man axed Jack to come in and put up with him for the night, and such poor accommodation as he had, Jack was heartily welcome to them. Jack thanked him and went in and put up the night with him, and in the morning Jack told the ould man the arrand he was on and axed if he'd diract him on his way to the Queen of the

Golden Mines's Castle. Then the ould man took out Jack, and showed him a copper castle glancing in the sun, on a hill opposite, and told him that was his journey's end. "But, my poor man," says he, "I would strongly advise ye not to go next or near it. A hundred knights went there afore you on the self-same errand, and their heads are now stuck on a hundred spears right afore the castle; for there's a fiery dragon guards it that makes short work of the best of them." But seeing Jack wasn't to be persuaded off his entherprise nohow, he took him in and gave him a sword that carried ten men's strength in it along with that of the man that wielded it. And he told Jack, if he was alive again' night, and not killed by the dhragon, to come back to his cabin. Jack thanked him for the sword, and promised this, and then he set out for the castle. But lo! and behold ye, no sooner did Jack come anear the castle than a terrible great monsther of a dhragon entirely, the wildest ever Jack seen or heard tell of, come out from the castle, and he opened his mouth as wide as the world from side to side, and let a roar that started the old grey eagle on top of

Croaghpathrick mountain at home in Ireland. Poor Jack thrimbled from head to foot —and small wonder he did—but, not a bit daunted, he went on to meet the dhragon, and no sooner were they met than he to it and the dhragon to it, and they fought and sthrove long and hard, the wildest fight by far that poor Jack ever entered into, and they fought that way from early mornin' till the sun went down, at one time Jack seemin' to be gettin' the betther of the dhragon, and the next minute the dhragon gettin' the betther of Jack; and when the sun went down they called a truce of peace till next day; and Jack dragged himself back to the cabin in small hopes of being able to meet the dhragon more, for he was covered over with wounds from head to foot. But when he got to the cabin the ould man welcomed him back alive, and he took down a little bottle of ointment and rubbed it over Jack, and no sooner did he rub it over him than Jack's wounds were all healed as well as ever again. And Jack went out a new man the next mornin' to give the dhragon another try for it this day. And just as on the

day afore the fiery dhragon come down the hill
meeting poor Jack; and the dhragon opened his
mouth as wide as the world, and gave a roar
that shook the nails on the toes of the great
grey eagle on top of Croaghpathrick mountain
at home in Ireland, and then he fell on Jack,
and Jack fell on him, and the dhragon
to it, and Jack to it; and the dhragon
gave Jack his fill, and Jack gave the
dhragon his fill; and if they fought hard the
day afore they fought double as hard this day,
and the dhragon put very sore on Jack entirely
till the sun went down. Then again they agreed
on a truce of peace till the next mornin', and
Jack dragged himself back as best he could to
the cabin again, all covered over with cuts and
bruises, and streaming down with blood. And
when he came there the ould man took down a
little bottle of ointment and rubbed Jack over
with it, and he was healed as well as ever again.
Next morning Jack was up quite fresh and
ready for another day's battling, and the ould
man told Jack that, win or lose, this day was
like to end the battle. And he said if Jack happened (as God send) to come off victorious, he

was to go into the castle, and there he would
find a great number of beautiful virgins running about in great confusion to prevent Jack
from discovering their mistress the Queen of
the Golden Mines, and every one of them axing,
"Is it me ye want? Is it me ye want?" But he
told Jack he was to heed none of them, but press
through room after room till he come to the
sixth room, and there he would find the Queen
herself asleep, with the little child by her side.
So Jack went meeting the dhragon this third
day again, and the dhragon come meeting Jack.
And he opened his mouth as wide as the world,
and let a roar that rattled the eyes in the sockets
of the great grey eagle on top of Croaghpathrick mountain at home in Ireland, and then fell
on Jack, and Jack fell on him; and he to it,
and Jack to it, and both of them to it;
and if the fight was wild and terrible
the first two days it was ten times
wilder and terribler this day. And harder
and harder it was getting the more they
warmed to the work; and one time it was Jack
was getting the better of the dhragon, and the
next time it was the dhragon was getting the

better of poor Jack; and at last coming on tor'st
night the dhragon was putting very hard on
Jack entirely, and it was very nearly being all
over with him, when he stepped back, and gathering all his strength mounted into the air with
one spring, and come down atop of the dhragon's head, and struck his sword into his heart,
leaving him over dead. Then Jack went
into the castle, and no sooner did he go
in than there was lots of the most beautiful virgins, running in great commotion, and asking Jack, "is it me ye want?" "Is it me ye
want?" But Jack never heeded thim till he
come into the sixth room, where he saw the
beautiful Queen of the Golden Mines asleep,
with the Queen of France's child asleep beside
her. Jack bent over her and gave her one kiss,
for she was a lovely picthur. Then he took up
the child in his arms, and picking up a beautiful
garter all glancing with diamonds, that was lying by the Queen's bedside, and taking with
him a loaf of bread that could never be eaten
out, a bottle of wine that could never be drunk
out, and a purse that could never be emptied, he
started away. He stopped that night with the

ould man, who took down his bottle of ointment
and healed up all the wounds Jack got that day.
In the morning Jack started for France, leaving
with the ould man to keep till the Queen of the
Golden Mines would call for it the purse that
never could be emptied.   When Jack reached
France, and presented back to the Queen her
darling child, that was the rejoicement and the
joy!   There was a great faist given, and at the
faist Jack said he had a little wondher he
fetched with him, that he'd like to show; and
he produced his bottle, and sent it round the
prences, and nobility, and genthry that were all
assembled at the faist, and axed them all to
drink the Queen's health out of it.   This they
all did; and lo! and behold ye, when they had
finished the bottle was as full as when they
commenced; and they all said that bate all ever
they knew or heerd tell of; and the King said
it bate all ever he knew or heerd tell of, too,
and that the same bottle would be of mighty
great sarvice to him, to keep his troops in drink
when he'd go to war, and axed Jack on what
tarms he'd part with it.   Jack said he couldn't
part with it entirely, as it wasn't his own, but

if the King relaised his brother he'd leave the
bottle with him till such times as the Queen of
the Golden Mines might call for it. The Queen
agreed to this. Jack's brother was relaised,
and himself and Jack started off for England.
When they were come there the King of England gave a great faist in their honour, too, and
at this faist Jack said he'd like to show them a
little wonder he fetched with him, and he produced the loaf, and axed the King to divide all
round. And the King cut off the loaf, and di-
vided all round, over all the prences and nobility
and gentry that was there; and when he had finished they were all lost in wondherment, for
the loaf was still as big as when the King commenced to cut. The King said that would be
the grand loaf for feeding his troops whenever
he went to war, and axed Jack what would he
take to part with it. Jack said the loaf wasn't
his to part with, but if the King relaised his
brother out of prison he'd give him the loaf till
such times as the Queen of the Golden Mines
might call for it. The King agreed to this,
and relaised Jack's other brother, and then the
three of them started for home together. And

when they were come near home the two older
brothers agreed that Jack when he'd tell his
story would disgrace them, and they'd put him
to death. But Jack agreed if they'd let him live
he would go away and push his fortune, and
never go back near home. They let him live on
these conditions, and they pushed on home,
where they were received with great welcomes,
and told mortial great things entirely of all the
great things they done while they were away.
Jack come to the castle in disguise and got hired
as a boy and lived there.

The Queen of the Golden Mines, when she
woke up and learned of the young gentleman
that had killed the dhragon, and carried off the
child and the other things, and kissed her, said
he must be a fine fellow entirely, and she would
never marry another man if she couldn't find
him out. She got no rest till she started, herself and her virgins, and away to find out Jack.
She first come to the old man, where she got
her purse, and he directed her to the King of
France. When she come to the Coort of the
King of France she got her bottle, and he said
Jack went from there to go to see the King of

England. From the King of England she got
her loaf, and he diracted her to Ireland, telling
her that Jack was no other than the King of
Ireland's son. She lost no time then reaching
the court of the King of Ireland, where she demanded his son who had killed the fiery dhragon. The King sent out his eldest son, and he
said it was him that had killed the fiery dhragon, and she asked him for tokens, but he could
give none, so she said he wasn't the man she
wanted. Then the King's second son come out
and said it was him killed the fiery dhragon.
But he couldn't show her no tokens either, so he
wouldn't do. Then the King said he had no
other son, but a good-for-nothing *droich* who
went away somewhere and never come back;
but that it wasn't him anyhow, for he couldn't
kill a cockroach. She said she'd have to see
him, and converse with him, or otherwise she
wouldn't go away till she'd pull down his castle.
Then the whole house was upside down, and
they didn't know what to do. And Jack, who
was doing something about the yards axed
what it was all about; and they told him, and
he axed to have a minute's convarsing with

her. But they all laughed at him; and one gave him a knock, and another gave him a push, and another gave him a kick. And Jack never minded them one bit, but went out and said it was him that kilt the fiery dhragon. They all set up another big roar of a laugh at this. Then the Queen asked him to show his tokens, and Jack fetched from his pocket the beautiful garter, all shining with jewels, and held it up, and the Queen came and threw her arms about Jack's neck and kissed him, and said he was the brave man she'd marry, and no other. And my brave Jack, to the astonishment of them all, confessed who he was, and got married to her, and was ever afther the King of the Golden Mines.

The Widow's Daughter

THE WIDOW'S DAUGHTER

THERE was once a poor widow woman, living in the North of Ireland, who had one daughter named Nabla. And Nabla grew up both idle and lazy, till at length, when she had grown to be a young woman, she was both thriftless and useless, fit only to sit with her heels in the ashes and croon to the cat the day long. Her mother was annoyed with her, so that one day, when Nabla refused to do some little trifle about the house, her mother got out a good stout sallyrod and came in and thrashed her soundly with it.

As her mother was giving Nabla the whacking she had so richly earned, who should happen to be riding past but the King's son himself. He heard the mother walloping and scolding, and Nabla crying and pleading within. So he drew rein, and at the top of his voice shouted to

know what was the matter. The widow came
to the door, curtseying when she saw who he
was. Not wishing to give out a bad name on
her daughter, she told the King's son that she
had a daughter who killed herself working the
leelong day and refused to rest when her
mother asked her, so that she had always to be
beaten before she would stop.

"What work can your daughter do?" the
Prince asked.

"She can spin, weave and sew, and do every
work that ever a woman did," the mother replied.

Now, it so happened that a twelvemonth
before the Prince had taken a notion of marry-
ing, and his mother, anxious he should have
none but the best wife, had, with his approval,
sent messengers over all Ireland to find him a
woman who could perform all a woman's du-
ties, including the three accomplishments the
widow named—spinning, that is, weaving and
sewing. But all the candidates whom the messengers had secured were found unsatisfactory
on being put to trial, and the Prince had re-
mained unwedded. When, now, the King's son

heard this account of Nabla from her own
mother he said:

" You are not fit to have the charge of such a
good girl.   For twelve months, through all
parts of my mother's kingdom, search was being made for just such a young woman that she
might become my wife.   I'll take Nabla with
me."

Poor Nabla was rejoiced and her mother as-
tonished.   The King's son helped Nabla to a
seat behind him on the horse's back and bidding
adieu to the widow rode off.

When he had got Nabla home, he introduced
her to his mother, telling the Queen that by
good fortune he had secured the very woman
they had so long sought in vain.   The Queen
asked what Nabla could do, and he replied that
she could spin, weave and sew, and do everything else a woman should; and, moreover, she
was so eager for work that her mother was
flailing her within an inch of her life to make
her rest herself when he arrived on the scene at
Nabla's own cottage.   The Queen said that
was well.

She took Nabla to a large room and gave her

a heap of silk and a golden wheel, and told her she must have all the silk spun into thread in twenty-four hours.   Then she bolted her in.

Poor Nabla, in amazement, sat looking at the big heap of silk and the golden wheel.   And at length she began to cry, for she had not spun a yard of thread in all her life.   As she cried an ugly woman, having one of her feet as big as a bolster, appeared before her.

" What are you crying for ? " she asked.

Nabla told her, and the woman said, " I'll spin the silk for you if you ask me to the wedding."

" I'll do that," Nabla said.   And then the woman sat down to the wheel, and working it with her big foot, very soon had the whole heap spun.

When the Queen came and found all spun she said : " That is good."   Then she brought in a golden loom and told Nabla she must have all that thread woven in twenty-four hours.

When the Queen had gone Nabla sat down and looked from the thread to the loom and from the loom to the thread, wondering, for she had not in all her life even thrown a shuttle. At

length she put her face in her hands and began
to cry.   There now appeared to her an ugly
woman with one hand as big as a pot hanging
by her side.   She asked Nabla why she cried.
Nabla told her, and then the woman said,

"I'll weave all that for you if you'll give me
the promise of your wedding."

Nabla said she would surely.   So the woman
sat down to the golden loom, and very soon had
all the thread woven into webs.

When again the Queen came and found all
woven she said: "That is good."   And then
she gave Nabla a golden needle and thimble and
said that in twenty-four hours more she must
have all the webs made into shirts for the
Prince.

Again when the Queen had gone, Nabla, who
had never even threaded a needle in all her life,
sat for a while looking at the needle and thimble
and looking at the webs of silk.   And again she
broke down, and began to cry heartily.

As she cried an ugly woman with a mons-
trously big nose came into the room and asked:

"Why do you cry?"

When Nabla had told her, the ugly woman said :

" I'll make up all those webs into shirts for the Prince if you promise me the wedding."

" I'll do that," Nabla said, " and a thousand welcomes."

So the woman with the big nose, taking the needle and thimble, sat down, and in a short time had made all the silk into shirts and disappeared again.

When the Queen came a third time and found all the silk made up in shirts she was mightily pleased and said :

" You are the very woman for my son, for he'll never want a housekeeper while he has you."

Then Nabla and the Prince were betrothed, and on the wedding night there was a gay and a gorgeous company in the hall of the Castle. All was mirth and festivity. But as they were about to sit down to a splendid repast there was a loud knock at the door. A servant opened it and there came in an ugly old woman with one foot as big as a pot who, amid the loud laughter of the company, hobbled up the floor and took a seat at the table. She was asked of which party was she, the bride or the groom's, and she replied that she was of the bride's party. When the Prince heard this he believed that she was one of Nabla's poor friends. He went up to her and asked her what had made her foot so big. "Spinning," she said, "I have been all my life at the wheel, and that's what it has done for me." "Then, by my word," said the Prince, striking the table a great blow, "my wife shall not turn a wheel while I'm here to prevent it!"

As the party were again settling themselves another knock came to the door. A servant opening it, let in a woman with one hand as big as a stool. The weight of this hand hanging by her side gave her body a great lean over, so that as she hobbled up the floor the company at the table lay back, laughing and clapping their hands at the funny sight. This woman, taking a seat at the table, was asked by whose invitation she was there, to which she replied that she was of the bride's party. Then the Prince went up to her and inquired what caused her hand to be so big.

"Weaving," she said. "I have slaved at the shuttle all my life; that's what has come on me."

"Then," the Prince said, striking the table a thundering blow, "by my word, my wife shall never throw a shuttle again while I live to prevent it."

A third time the company were ready to begin their repast, when again there came a knock to the door. Every one looked up; and they saw the servant now admit an ugly old woman with the most monstrous nose ever beheld. This woman likewise took a chair at the table. She was then asked who had invited her—the bride or the groom. She said she was one of the bride's party. Then the Prince, going up to her, asked her why her nose had come to be so very big.

"It's with sewing," she said. "All my life I have been bending my head over sewing, so that every drop of blood ran down into my nose, swelling it out like that."

Then the Prince struck the table a blow that made the dishes leap and rattle.

"By my word," he said, "my wife shall

never either put a needle in cloth again or do any other sort of household work while I live to prevent it."

And the Prince faithfully kept his word. He was always on the lookout to try and catch Nabla spinning, weaving or sewing, or doing any other sort of work, for he thought she might at any time try to work on the sly.

Poor Nabla, however, never did anything to confirm his uneasiness, but, taking her old mother to stop in the Castle with her, lived happy and contented, and as lazy as the day was long, ever after.

Shan Ban and Ned Flynn

SHAN BAN AND NED FLYNN

SHAN BAN and Ned Flynn were neighbour-
ing farmers that wrought hard on their wee
bits of farms to support themselves and their
wives—but that same was more nor they could
do; so says Shan Ban to Ned Flynn one day,
"Ned," says he, "what do ye think if we start
off to push our fortunes, and leave our wives
to look out for themselves for a while?"
"Why, I think," says Ned, says he, "it wouldn't
be a bad idea at all." No sooner sayed than
done, off both of them starts, and away afore
them to push their fortunes. They thravelled
away for the length of a day, without meeting
with anything remarkable, and long afther
night fell on them they were still wanderin' on
when Shan sees a light away from him, and
"Ned," says he, "I think we'll dhraw on that
light." Well and good, on the light they

dhrew, and when they come there, they found
the light was shining from a great castle, and
in they went to the castle, and finding or seeing
no one there, they wandhered on through it
from room to room, dumfoundered with all the
gorgeous grandeur, goold an' silver, they saw
everywhere. At last they come to a great din-
ing-room, with a great dinner entirely, of all
sorts of the richest and grandest, and nicest
eating and drinking spread out on the tables.
"Come, help ourselves," says Shan, "we'll line
our insides anyhow." "A good job," says Ned;
and both of them fell to, and made a hearty
meal. Then all at once they heard music and
the tramping of feet coming tor'st them. "We'll
have to hide," says Shan; and "I think it's
best," says Ned. So both of them took and hid
themselves under a sofa where they couldn't be
seen. Ned wasn't right under the sofa when he
was fast asleep by reason of the big dinner he
ate. But Shan kept wide awake, and peeping
out through a little hole in the sofa cloth could
see all that was going on. Into the room came
a company of five hundred fairies, little men
and women, all grandly dressed in every colour

of silks and satins and ribbons, with forty little
pipers playing before them, and they dancing
along behind with their hands caught. When
they come in, the forty pipers played three times
round the dinner table till the rest of the company bowed to one another and got saited, and
then the pipers laid aside their pipes and sat
down themselves. Afther they had made a
good dinner the decanthers of all sorts of
whiskies and wines and rare drinks was put on
the table, and then the little man that sat at the
head give it out that every one present would
have to sing a song, crack a joke, or tell a good
tale. And round the table at once went the
singing and the joking and the telling of the
stories. Says one of the fairies, "I'll tell a
good story;" and he begun to tell how the
King's daughter was lying very ill, and all the
great doctors of the country was attending to
her; but it was all no use, for she was pining
away day afther day under the fairies' spells,
and there was nothing in the world could save
her except three mouthfuls of the dandylion
which grew on the Grey Forth, and which had
the virtue of curing all diseases. Shan Ban's

heart jumped when he heard this, and he waited
patiently till, when day was going to break, the
pipers got up and took their pipes, and the company got up, and the pipers played afore them
out of the room, and the fairies danced out
afther. Then Shan wakened up Ned, and taking him with him went out and up the Grey
Forth, plucked the dandylion that grew there,
never letting on to Ned what he meant
by it, and both of them started away for
the King's palace. When they were come there
they knocked, and the sarvints axed them what
they wanted, and Shan said he had come to try
and cure the King's daughter. The sarvints of
course only laughed at Shan, but the King hearing of him ordered him to be brought up. And
when Shan was brought up into the princess's
bed-chamber there that place was filled with great
doctors, and when they heard Shan was coming
to try to cure the princess they laughed hearty.
But the King said they had their try and
made nothing of it, and that Shan Ban might
as well get his try, for he couldn't have worse
luck nor them anyhow. Then Shan ordered
all the doctors out of the room, and giving the

princess one mouthful of the dandylion she got great aise entirely, then he gave her another mouthful, and she felt a deal better still; then he gave her the third mouthful, and she was completely cured. There was great rejoicement entirely at this, and the King in particular was beside himself with delight and offered Shan Ban the prencess in marriage. But Shan wouldn't have her on no account, for he said he wouldn't part his wife Molly at home for all the princesses in the world, no matter how beautiful they might be. Then the King filled two bags, one with goold and the other with silver, and give them to Shan. When Shan got outside the castle he handed the two bags to Ned and told him to take them home with him, and give his (Shan's) wife the bag of goold and keep the bag of silver for himself; and that he wouldn't go home himself till he would thravel further and see were there any more adventures. Then both of them parted, Ned for home with the bags of money and Shan travelling away further before him. Shan travelled on that day till at night falling he was getting into a wood, when what does he see sitting on a sycamore leaf but the identical same little fairy that told at the supper the story about the King's daughter. "Shan Ban, Shan Ban," says the little fellow, "you hid and listened to our stories the other night and heard me tell the secret of the King's daughter and the dandylion on the Grey Forth, and then ye went and cured the princess. What did ye do that for?" "Well, small blame to me," says Shan, "I had to hide, and I couldn't help hearing yer story; and sure I'd be an onnatural man, out and out, if I didn't save the poor princess's life when I had it in my power to do it so aisy. Small blame to me, I say again," says Shan. "Well, that's surely true," says the fairy, "but that's a mighty great saicret, that about the dandylion, and if it got out it's I would be blamed for it, and I would never hear the last of it nor get any living afther from the rest of the fairies, and I would be made a miserable devil entirely." "Well, if that's so," says John, "the saicret's a saicret yet, for man or mortial didn't hear it from me; and if it's a consolation to ye I promise ye it'll be so." "Thanky, very much," says the fairy; "it's certainly a conso-

lation and a great one, and I know I may de-
pend on yer promise. And, when you're so
mighty kind, Shan Ban," says he, "I'll be
every bit as kind. Here's a napkin for ye that
ye have only to spread it out and wish for what
ye like, and as much as ye like, of aitables and
drinkables, and immediately they will be placed
on it. And here's a wishing cap," says he, "ye
have only to put on yer head and wish to be any
place in the world ye like, and immediately ye'll
be there. And here's a purse filled with money,
that no matther how much ye take out of it it
will never get empty." He handed over to
Shan the napkin, the wishing cap, and the
purse, and then disappeared without even waiting to be thanked. Shan was feeling just hungry enough, and he spread out the napkin to try
it. He wished for a nice supper for himself,
and, lo and behold ye! all at once there
was the rarest supper, aiting and drinking, ever he laid his two eyes on, spread
on the napkin. He ate and drunk heartily,
and then spread himself out under the
trees to sleep. In the morning Shan got up and
spread his napkin and wished for a breakwus,

and had the finest of aiting and drinking again,
his hearty fill, and then he set off on his journey
once more. Tor'st evening he was travelling in a very bare and barren country, without
any people, or anything growing that a man
could ate, or anything flowing that a man
could drink. And here, as he spread his
napkin and had a beautiful dinner on it,
who should come up to him, weary and worn,
but a piper: and John axed him to sit
down and help him with dinner. Nothing
loath, down the piper sat, for he was
most dead with the hunger; and both of them
ate as good a dinner as ever they ate in their
lives afore. When they were finished the piper
pulled out a horn, and commenced to play his
pipes, and four hundred thousand troopers—
Light Dhragoons, Heavy Dhragoons, Hussians, Grenadiers, and Kilties—come troopin'
out of the horn, and begun dancing to the music. Then the piper told Shan he was under
great distress entirely, because for the last five
days, being in this barren country, he hadn't a
bit to put in the mouths of his troopers, and
they were dying with hunger. Then says Shan,

"I'll soon relieve them," and he spread his napkin and wished for aiting and drinking for four
hundred thousand troopers, and immaidiately
it was on the napkin, and the troopers all ate
and drunk to their satisfaction, and went in to
the horn again. "Well, says the piper, "that
is a wondherful great napkin entirely, and I
wouldn't care if I had it instead of my horn of
troopers—for what use are they to me if I can't
feed them?"   "I'll swap with ye, the napkin for
the horn," says Shan.   "Done," says the piper,
and handing over to Shan the horn, he took the
napkin and started off.   But when my brave
Shan found himself in possession of the horn
and four hundred thousand troopers he axed
himself how was he going to get them fed at
all, at all.   And says he, "If I only had the napkin now to feed them I'd be a happy man."   At
once he ordhered the troopers out of the horn,
and they come tumbling out, Light Dhragoons,
Heavy Dhragoons, Hussians, Grenadiers, and
Kilties, and away he sent them after the piper
to take the napkin from him.   And when they
brought Shan the napkin he ordered them again
into their horn, and said he'd now go for home.

So he put the wishing cap on his head and wished to be home. And when he got there and looked about him he couldn't know it was the same country at all, at all, for there, in the place where Ned Flynn's house used to be, was a great castle with gardens, and lawns, and parks all round it. He come up to the door of his own house, and Molly was the glad woman to see him back. "And what," says he to Molly, "is the meanin' of that great castle where Ned Flynn's cabin used to be?" "Oh," says Molly, says she, "sure Ned Flynn was away, no one knows where, pushing his fortune, and he come home with no end of bags of money with him, and had up that grand castle and all them parks and lawns before ye'd have time to look about ye. He's now very rich entirely, and, doesn't know his own wealth." "And Molly," says Shan, "was he any way kind to you when he come back with so much money, or did he make ye ever a present?" "Kind!" says Molly; "kind's no name for it. He give me five shillings the day afther he come home, and has ordhered me an' allowance of half-a-crown a week ever since." Says Shan,

"I must set off to see him." "Oh, no, ahasky,
Shan," says Molly, ye couldn't go to see him in
them old clothes, or he'd ordher you to be shot."
But Shan set off to Ned Flynn's castle, and
when he was come there he inquired of the servants to see Lord Flynn. But they told him
they couldn't let him into his lordship's presence at all, at all, in such old clothes as he had
on him. But Lord Flynn heard that Shan Ban
was at the door wanting to get in to see him,
and he ordhered the servants to let him in and
bring him upstairs to him. He shook hands
heartily with Shan, and said he was glad to see
him home again. John thanked him, and said
his wife, Molly, was telling him that he had
been very good to her, and he thanked him entirely for this. Then Lord Flynn said he was
going to give a great ball, and, to show he had
no ill-will again' Shan, axed himself and his
wife to come to it. Shan and Molly attended the
ball, and then axed Lord Flynn and his wife to
come to their house to a ball next night. When
Shan got home, says Molly to him, says she,
"Shan, do ye intend enthertaining Lord Flynn
and his wife? Sure ye haven't a proper house

to take them to; nor ye have no money to buy
provisions to enthertain them properly." "Oh,
we'll soon rightify that," says Shan. He took
out the purse and covered the floor with gold,
and filled up a room full of it. He then ordhered
out his four hundred thousand troopers out of
the horn, and set them to work building a great
castle, and before the next night he had the
castle up, and all its walls lined with silver, and
its floors of beaten gold, and he had a gold walk
right from the door of it to Lord Flynn's castle.
And when Lord Flynn and his wife come they
were all in wondherment and didn't know what
to make of it at all. And Shan Ban and Molly
welcomed them, and they dressed up in the most
gorgeous dresses, and Molly with two diamonds
hanging from her ears, the size of turf.   Then
there was no end of sarvints in waiting, and the
napkin was spread, and Shan wished for the
grandest supper that ever was, and immediately
the grandest that ever was seen, afore or since,
was before them.   And when Lord Flynn got
home, he sent a messenger to the King to tell
him of the wondherful napkin Shan Ban had,
and that it would be of great sarvice to the

King in times of war, and axed the King
to send his sojers for it. So the King
sent thirty sojers to demand the napkin
of Shan; but Shan turned out sixty
sojers out of his horn who fell on the
King's sojers and killed them all but one, who
went home and told the King. Then the King
sent ten thousand troopers; but Shan turned
fifty thousand troopers out of the horn, and
killed all the King's men to one, again.
Then the King sent a hundred thousand
troopers; and Shan now turned out of
the horn his four hundred thousand
troopers—Light Dhragoons, Heavy Dhragoons, Hussians, Grenadiers, and Kilties,
and they fell on the King's men, and not
one of them at all, at all, escaped this time.
Then the King come to parley with Shan, and
he made paice with him, and said it was Lord
Flynn who had told him about the napkin, and
put him up to taking it from Shan. So Shan
once again turned out his troopers—Light
Dhragoons, Heavy Dhragoons, Hussians,
Grenadiers, and Kilties—and ordhered them up
to Lord Flynn's to blow up his castle and not

lay a trace of him or his on the earth.   And
this they did, and Lord Flynn and his wife were
killed, and Shan Ban and Molly, spent the remainder of their days ever afther in paice and
plinty.

When Neil a-Mughan was Tuk

WHEN NEIL A-MUGHAN WAS TUK

WE had been in the middle of our story-tell-in', with all our seats drawn close together round Shemishin's big hearth fire. The storm of rain and sleet without gave us no bother, only made us enjoy the comfort of the big fire, and the great stories, far more keenly. But in the middle of an excitin' story of Paudeen Mor's—a fearful adventure of his in the wilds of Georgia, when he was carrying the pack there, the latch rattled, and the door burst open, and into the middle of the floor stepped a man, with a scared look on his face, and out of whose clinging clothes, streams of water were running, and pouring over the floor. The wet hair came down his brows and fell in wet tongues, and streams were running from it. His hat leaf drooped over all like a limp rag.

"God bliss all here!" he said.

"And yerself likewise," we said, when we got our breaths.

"Thank God!" said he from his heart. "It's me is the glad man to get a Christian roof over me head. I've been tuk."

"What? By the fairies? On such a night?"

"The fairies," Shemishin said, rebuking us, "wouldn't take any Christun on such a night."

"They wouldn't," said the stranger, "and didn't. I was tuk by Willie-the-Wisp."

"God help ye, poor man," Shemishin said, "ye had a narrow escape." And, "God help ye, poor man," we all said, and made room for him amongst us.

"I'm Neil a-Mughan of Tievahurkey," said he. "I was comin' from Donegal where I was in payin' the rent to Misther Martin. It was mortial dark an' I feared I'd lose me way. Two mile back I seen the light in from me, an' I dhrew on it thinkin' of course it was a house. An' as I stumbled on, it seemed farther and farther away. I was gettin' deeper in the mire at every step I tuk, but I sthruggled on for the dear life to reach that light. I darsay it tuk me a long mile, among such marshes and bog-holes that only God willed it, and I had some poor body's prayer about me, I couldn't have escaped with the life. Three times runnin' I was steppin' intil a bog-hole when somethin' (I thought) toul' me not to lay down me foot —I held it back, and looked, and the black bottomless wather lay right at me toe—"

"Musha, God was by ye."

"He was. Thanks be till Him, this night."—

"Amen! Amen!"

"Well, when I'd gone the full mile, an' seen I was only gettin' more hopelesser into the bog, it sthruck me like a flash that it was no other nor Willie-the-Wisp, and all at wanst, I seen how I'd been deluded and a'most lost. But there I was in the middle of a black threacherous bog in a night as sleety and wet as sorra, and as dark as the inside of a cow, an' where the next step might mean death. I turned, as nearly as I could think, in the same direction I had come—an' yous may take my word for it that I was prayin' faster nor I was used to. If I have any idea of time that's two solid hours ago—and here I am now! This is the first sign of Christianity I've seen. How I got out of the

bog is more nor I can tell meself—only I know
God (praise be till Him!) was guidin' me
steps."

Poor Norah, when she recovered sufficiently
from the shock of both the stranger's appearance, and his story, warmed him a skillet of
milk, and literally insisted on pouring it down
the poor fellow's throat when it must have felt
like so much molten lead. But Norah would
hear of no remonstrance, and Shemishin,
equally well-intentioned, stood by and held the
victim.

Neil a-Mughan survived. Then Norah turned
Patrick Burns's only sons Charlie and Ned out
of the chimney-corner in which they squatted,
and stuck Neil into it—"till the hait gets in
about yer heart," she said, "and dhrives all the
sleet out of yer bones." She put on what she
called "a pitcher of tay," for him, then but-
tered several large fadges of oaten bread, and
boiled four eggs hard, and gave all to him in
the corner.

Neil felt a new man as he got around these;
and by sympathy our spirits got higher, too,
and we felt in the mood to hear Shemishin

(than whom there were few better fitted to do it) give us the story of Willie-the-Wisp, and the reason for his wanderings, and his evil tricks upon travellers:—

In the grand old times, long, long ago, there was wanst a blacksmith, and his name was Willie—and he was notorious over all Ireland for the dhrinkin' sportin' way he spent all of his life—and it was often and often prophesied for him that he'd never come till a good ending. He had come of good family, and besides his thrade—which was in them days, a profession for a gentleman—his people had left to him great properties both in houses and in lands. But all these properties Willie very soon dhrunk and sported away,—and all melted like snow in summer. When it come to that he had only his trade, Willie had purty hard times of it; for he didn't want to work, and he didn't care to starve,—and he found it purtikilarly hard to have no money to sport and spend, as he was used to do. He worked as little as he could, but he wanted as much as ever; so things went on from bad to worse, and his chances of thrade even was laivin' him, for no man could be sartin whether he'd oblige them or refuse them (accordingly as the mood was on him) when they'd bring a horse to shoe, or a plough to mend. And at long and at last wan mornin' that he had got no breakfast, bekase he had neither money nor means, he was standin' leanin' against his own forge doore, with his heart in his boots, when what should come up the road but a poor miserable lookin' old fella with a pair of broken pot-hooks in his hand and, "Good man," says he to Willie, would ye mind doin' a little job for me, and mendin' these pot-hooks?" Willie was in ill-humour for workin'; but with all his faults he had always a soft spot for the poor somewhere or other in his heart. So when he looks at the little ragged man and his broken pot-hooks for a minute, he says, "Step inside," an' takin' the pieces out of the old man's hand, he blew up the fire, an' very soon made the pot-hooks all right again. "How much for that?" says the wee old man. But Willie was mad with him for mentionin' a charge. "Well thanky, thanky," says the wee

fella, "It's little money I'd have to offer ye anyhow. But since ye are so kind-hearted I'll not
laive ye without givin' ye some reward. Ax
me," says he, "for any three requests ye like—
barrin' money or money's worth, an' I'll give
them to ye." Willie at wanst seen that he was
dailin' with a fairy. "Well," says Willie,
"there's a lot of lazy loungers comes about me
house an' forge, an' annoy me tarribly throwin'
me sledge, an' sittin' themselves down in me
armchair, an' sometimes even bein' so dishonest
as to pick the very money out of me purse—
when there's any in it. So I wish," says Willie,
"first that anywan ever takes up that sledge
cannot laive it down again without I let them;
and I wish anywan sits down in my armchair
mayn't be able to rise from it, till I allow them:
and I wish that once a piece of money goes into
my purse, it can't get out again till I take it
out." " Yer wishes is granted, Willie," says the
wee old man, "an' I'm sorry ye didn't wish for
health, happiness, and Heaven," and he went
away.

Then Willie was standin' leanin' in his forge-
doore again ruminatin' over it all, and feelin'

far more down-hearted than afore, when all at
wanst he hears the noise of hoofs, and up there
rides a grand gentleman entirely mounted on a
great black charger. And "Helloa, Willie," says
he, "what are ye so down in the mouth about
this mornin'?   Ye look as lorn as a March
graveyard." "Small wonder I would," says Willie, says he.   "And if you had the same raison
it's not such a spruce jaunty lookin' gentleman
you'd be this mornin'." "I'm mortial sorry for
ye Willie," says the gentleman.   "Can I help
ye?" "I dar'say ye could; but I don't expect
ye would," says Willie. "Don't be so sartin of
that," says the gentleman—"What is it ye
need?" "Money," says Willie, "an' plenty of
it." "How much of it?" says the gentleman.
"Och, a roomful," says Willie that way, care-
less. "Well, a roomful," says the gentleman,
says he, "you'll have,—on wan condition."
"And what is the condition?" says Willie, says
he, brightenin' up.   "It's this," says the gentleman, "that you'll consent to give yerself to me
and come with me in seven years and a
day from now." At this Willie's eye
went down and caught sight of one of

the gentleman's feet an' he seen it was cloven. "Phew!" says Willie, says he, "is that how the hare sits?" "It's a grand offer," says the gentleman. "Just this minute ye were plannin' how ye'd do away with yerself. It's cowl' comfort to go out of the wurrl' on a hungry belly. Here ye have the offer of a roomful of money, an' a whole year to spend and sport it. Think of all the fun ye'd get out of a roomful of money in twelvemonths and a day!" "Thrue for ye," says Willie: "it's a bargain."

Without another word then, the Devil filled with goold the biggest room in Willie's house. "And now," says he, "good-bye, and be ready for me in seven years and a day from now." "I'll be ready," says Willie.

Willie had a gay and a rollickin' time and no mistake, afther that, for the seven years and a day. He made the money spin, as it was never afore known to spin in Ireland. He come to be known all over the country as the greatest sporter and spender of the day. He kept race horses, and stee-ple-chase horses, carriages and coaches—

and everything was thrapped out in solid goold. He built castles that had a window for every day of the year—and entertained Kings in them. And bards and chiefs were as plentiful about them as rats. The fame of the great rich blacksmith spread over the known wurrl' of them days, and great distinguished tourists and genthry of all descriptions come flockin' from all arts and parts to see him, and to receive his hospitality—bekase he kept open house for all comers, and sarvints to wait on them, and coaches and coach-horses to dhrive them.

But for all his wealth, Willie couldn't stop Time from runnin'. And at long and at last the seven years and a day's sparin's was up, an' as Willie was wan day sittin' down to a grand dinner entirely among Kings and Counts an' many l'arned people, and people of high degree, the door of the great dinin' hall opened, and a tall gentleman walked in. Willie looked up and at the first glint he remembered him. "Good morra, Willie," says the stranger. "I suppose you know me, and are ready for me." "Good-morra and good luck," says Willie, not a thrifle mismoved—"Yis, I know you, and I'm ready for ye—as soon as I get through with dinner (it would be bad manners to laive me guests at table) an' make a set of goold shoes that I've promised the King of Prooshia there below for his horse—let me inthroduce you to the King. —King," says Willie to the King, "this is"— "A frien'," says the Devil. "—A frien'," says Willie. An' the King an' the Devil bowed, the Devil remarkin' he hoped for the pleasure of a further acquaintance with him some day. He told Willie not to hurry, an' took his place at the table, and a right hearty dinner, and then went with Willie to the forge, to see him turn out the goold shoes. "Here," says Willie, says he, "when he was baitin' these out on the anvil, "make yerself useful, and help me through till I be off with ye"—handin' him a sledge. The Devil took hold of the sledge with both hands and begun baitin'; but the sarra wan of him could let it go when he wanted to, for the sledge stuck to his hands like grim daith. "Come," says Willie, says he, "old man, are ye ready for the road?" "Take away this sledge out of me

hands," says the Devil. "I don't recall," says
Willie, "that there's anything about that in my
bargain. I'm afeerd ye'll have to stick to the
sledge. Come along," says he, "I'm ready."
"Och, ye scoundhril," says the Devil, says he,
and he dancin' all over the place, with all Willie's guests and friends standin' by brakin'
their hearts laughin' at him. "Take away this
sledge," says he, at long and at last, "and I'll
give ye another seven years' and a day's
sparin's." So, at that Willie tuk from him the
sledge, and the Devil went off in mighty anger.

It was like new life to Willie startin' the next
tarm. And he went at these seven years of fun
and frolic, like a man at a day's work. And if
the seven years afore had been a merry seven,
these seven were seven times as merry. His
house never emptied, and day or night the fun
and carousin' never wanst ceased in it. There
come more throops and bands, and Kings and
Queens with all their body-sarvints than ever
went to visit Solomon in all his glory. His
name and fame was sounded in the utthermost
ends of the earth; and in all the wurrl' again
there wasn't so great a man as Willie.

But at long and at last, again, these seven years and a day passed, too. And on the very day when they were up, just as Willie, again, was sittin' down to table in the middle of Kings and Queens, and great foreign Counts, the doore of the dinin' hall opened and in steps no other than Willie's frien'. "Good morra, Willie," says he, with an ugly smile on his face as much as to say "I'm goin' to get even with ye at last, boy-o." "Good-morra, and good luck," says Willie, not the laist thrifle mismoved, seemin'ly. "Willie," says he, "I hope you're ready to come with me?" "I am," says Willie —"Butler," says Willie, "bring forrid that large chair there behind you and set it here at my right hand for this gentleman, and bring him in a large plate of the best ye can find in the pot—he's going to do us the honor of pickin' a bone with us." "Thanky, thanky," says the Devil, says he, seatin' himself, and tacklin' the dinner with a rale hearty appetite.

But lo, when all had finished their dinners, and Willie had sayed grace and stood up, the Devil he couldn't rise at all, at all, for he was

stuck as fast to the chair as if he had been
waxed to it. "I'm ready for the road now, old
man," says Willie,—are you?" "Oh, ye notorious villain," says the Devil, "this is a purty
mane thrick to play on a man in your own house,
and at your own table, moreover. Relaise me
from this chair," says he. "I don't remember
that there was anything about that in my bargain," says Willie. The Devil he wriggled and
wriggled, and screwed and twisted himself, till
all the gentlemen and ladies present went into
stitches with the laughin'. And then, says he,
"Relaise me out of this chair and I'll give ye
seven years and a day more." "Done," says
Willie; and he relaised him, and let him go off,
black in the countenance with anger and wrath.

Willie's pile of money was by no means as
big as what it used to be, but there was an
odious pile of it yet. And so for the next seven
years, Willie run the same rigs he had done
afore; only, if anything, he went it ten times
faster and furiouser, and his house was the
resort for ten times as many princes and people
from the very corners of the earth itself. And
the fun was ten times as big, and the aitin'

and dhrinkin' ten times as great and grand. And the likes of it never had been seen afore nor never will be seen again.

But the best of things must some time or other come till an end. And so it seemed with Willie; for these years passed, too. And the day the devil was due, come; and on that day, just as afore, Willie, he was sittin' down till the table to dinner, along with all his great distinguished guests, when the doore of the dinin' room opens, and in walks me brave Devil again. "Good morra, Willie," says he, with the same old vicious smile. "Good morra and good luck," says Willie, as little as ever mismoved, "won't ye sit down and have a pick of dinner with us?" "Not me," says the Devil. "You fooled me twicet, but ye'll never have it to say that ye fooled me the third time. Come along," says he. "That's mighty curt," says Willie. "It's your desarts," says the Devil. "Lay down the knife and fork now, and throt." And Willie had there and then to say good-bye to his guests, an' beg their pardon for this hasty departure, an' walk off, hungry as he was, with the Devil.

It was in the heat of summer, and the roads was dhry and dusty, and the sun burnin' down on top of the two thravellers. After they'd been some hours walkin' Willie complained he was mighty thirsty. "Well," says the Devil, says he, the first inn we come till, I'll let ye go in and have a dhrink." Says Willie, "But I haven't got a stiver on me, me purse is as emp'y as Micky Meehan's male-chist." "Neither have I a stiver," says the Devil. "What'll ye do?" "Why, as for that," says Willie, "You're such a nice obligin' fella that I know ye'll oblige me in this. All you've got to do is to turn yourself until a goold piece in my purse whilst I buy a thrait with ye." "I'll do that, with a heart and a half," says the Devil. And the first inn they come up till, the Devil thrans-formed himself intil a goold piece in Willie's purse, and Willie closed the purse on him. Then straight back home with him Willie marched and into his forge. He laid the purse down on the anvil, and gettin' two other sthrong lumps of fellas along with himself, he put sledges in their hands, and told them fire away and not spare themselves. So, as heavy and fast as the three of them could, they rained the blows down upon the purse on the anvil; and every blow come down, the Devil he yelled. And they struck away, and he yelled away; and he cried out and begged of Willie to let him out, and he'd give him more sparin's. And when Willie got all the fun himself and his friends needed for wan day, out of him, Willie released him from the purse, on his promisin' to give him seven years and a day more.

But poor Willie's money, which had been goin' all this time like corn in a sieve, was now run purty low. For six of the seven years he had as gay a time and as merry as ever afore—but the money run out with the sixth year, and poor Willie had no means of makin' more—for he'd sooner starve than work. His friends disappeared, too, with the money; and him that thought he could count friends be the thousand couldn't find as much as one single one, now, on lookin' round him. The seventh year, then, was a purty hard one with Willie; an' he was no ways sorry to find the end of it comin', and with it the Devil—for he had got heart-sick, sore, and tired, of the wurrl'.

And when at the end of the seventh year and a day the Devil come again he found Willie, with the stick in his fist waitin' him. And Willie started along with him this time with a heart and a half. And on ahead the both of them thrudged and thravelled for many a weary, dhreary mile, for further nor I could tell you, and twicet further nor you could tell me, till at long at last they reached their journey's end, and the Devil knocked on the gates of Hell, and had both of them admitted in.

But behold you, Willie wasn't long in here till he tired of it, and wished he was free again. So he set about makin' himself as bothersome as he could, and *yocked* a row with everybody in it, till they could stand him no longer, and put in a petition to the Devil to have him put out of here, bekase there'd never be no more comfort whilst he'd be let remain. And the Devil himself, too, found him so throublesome that he was only too glad to give in, and to ax the request of Willie that he'd go quietly, and

laive them in paice. But Willie was conthrary,
as always he had been, and he now refused to
go till they had to join and put him out by main
force. And when they got him out, and the
gates slammed on him, Willie kicked up a
racket outside, and pegged on the gates for all
he was worth, and wouldn't go away till they'd
consent to hand him out a torch, that he might
see his way by. So the Devil, through the
bars of the gate, handed out till him the torch,
and told him to begone back to the wurrl' he
come from, and spend his time ever afther in
leadin' good people asthray.

Back Willie come, and from that day to this,
he has continued wandherin' afore him, over
hill and dale, himself and his torch; and it's his
great delight to atthract the attention of good
people that have lost their way at night, and
lead them into marshes, and bogs, and swamps,
where they get stuck, and sunk, and lost.

And from that day to this, owin' to the torch
or wisp he carries in his hand, he has been called
Willie-the-Wisp. And on our friend Neil here
to-night he had evil intentions; but, as Neil re-
marked, he had some poor body's prayer on

him, and God reached till him a helpin' hand,
and led him out of the bog.

"Thank God!" we all said fervently.
And Neil said: "Thanks be to Him!"

The Black Bull of the Castle of Blood

THE BLACK BULL OF THE CASTLE OF BLOOD

ONCE on a time, long, long ago, when good people were scarcer, and enchantments more plentiful, there was a Queen who had three beautiful daughters who were renowned far and wide for their handsome looks and gentle ways, and were courted by kings and princes, and many others of high degree, but hadn't yet been won by any. One day a great prince, that no one knew, and who had never been seen in that country before, came, like the others, looking for the hand of one of these beautiful ladies. But the queen approved of him, in case he was able to succeed in winning the willing hand of either of her daughters, and though he tried his very best he couldn't win either of them; for they hadn't yet seen enough of him, and didn't know enough about him to consent, either of them, to be his for life. Then, he was too proud and too haughty to spend time in his courting, like the other great gentlemen who endeavoured to win them, and when he couldn't have his desire granted at once he would not delay, but went away from the queen's court in great wrath, saying angrily that the next time he came for them they would come with him without the asking.

It wasn't long after he went away, when one morning, the queen and her three daughters sitting by a window, chatting, and looking out on the lovely grounds, saw a great black bull tramping among, and rooting up their flower beds. They were greatly annoyed at this, and the eldest daughter jumped up and ran out, seizing a bit of stick by the way to drive the bull from the garden, but when she reached the bull and struck him with the stick, the stick stuck to the bull, and her hand stuck to the stick, so that she couldn't let it go. Then the bull started away, dragging her after him and over high hills, and low hills, grey mountains, and green plains he ran, with the lady still drawn after him, very soon disappearing from view of the queen's castle, and for three days and three

nights he never stopped running so, till he
reached another great castle, painted the colour
of blood. Here the bull changed into the
shape of a man, and the frightened young princess saw that he was no other than the haughty
prince they had a short time before rejected.

"Now lady," said he, "it was my last warn-
ing, when leaving your castle, that the next
time I would visit you, you would come with
me without being asked. You see, my word
was good, whether you will or no. I now make
you mistress of my castle. If you obey me you
shall want for nothing, and shall be happier than
even in your mother's. But if you ever dare
to disobey me, your fate will be that of many
unfortunate ones who went before you, and
whose blood has painted my castle the colour
you see it."

The princess resigned herself to her fate,
making herself as comfortable as she could that
night, and in the morning the prince came to
her with a great bunch of keys, which he gave
into her possession, saying:

"Now, since you are to be mistress of my
castle, I give you charge of all the keys of it. I

go away to remain away for a day, and you can
pass your time pleasantly going through the
castle and seeing all the beautiful rooms in it.
Only this—there," said he, pointing out
a key, "is one key, and do not use it, nor enter
the room it opens.   If you dare to do so, you
will surely suffer for your idle curiosity."

Then he went away, and the princess at her
leisure went through the rooms of the castle
one after another, admiring their beauty and
gorgeousness, until she had seen all but the forbidden room.   And when she came to it she
looked long at the door, and,

"Well now," she said, "I wonder what can be
in that room, or why he has forbidden me to
enter it.   I would like to see it; and why
mightn't I just turn the key and peep in? Who
can know?"

So she put the key in the door and turned it,
and seeing the floor covered with some red matter she put her foot in it and found it was blood.
Then she was horrified on looking round the
walls to see that it was hung all round with the
bodies of beautiful ladies, whom she then knew
the prince must have murdered.   Then she

quickly closed the room again, and locked it.
She went to wash the blood from her foot,
but found that no matter how much she tried,
though she rubbed it and scrubbed it in a running stream by the castle, that she could not
get even the smallest drop of the blood washed
out. But she thought she could easily hide
it from her lord, and went about her business
unconcerned. In the evening she took bread
and a basin of milk into the garden to have supper under the trees. As she drank the milk a
cat crept up to lick the drops that fell from the
bowl, but the princess struck the cat with her
foot.

"Miaow! Miaow!" said the cat. "If you
let me drink up only what milk you let drop, I
will lick half the blood off your foot."

"Get out," said she, kicking the cat again.
"How would you lick it off when I wasn't able
to wash it off myself."

Then a robin redbreast came hopping up,
picking the crumbs she let fall, and she threw a
stick at the robin.

"Toowhit! Toowhit!" said the robin, "If you
let me pick up what crumbs you let fall, I'll tell

how to take away one half the blood on your foot."

"Get out!" said she, throwing another stick at the robin. "When I couldn't wash it off myself how could you tell me?"

Next day the prince returned and asked for the keys. She gave them to him.

"I hope," he said, "you did not disobey me, and open the room I forbade you?"

"No," she said, "I did not."

"Show me your feet," said he.

She tried to hide the foot that was covered with blood, but it was no use, for the prince insisted on seeing it. And when he saw the blood upon it he had her killed and hung up in the secret room.

At the queen's castle there was great grief and great trouble at the loss of the princess, and on a morning about a week after she had been carried off, the queen and her two daughters sat by the window talking of their loss, when once more the black bull appeared in the garden rooting up the beautiful flowers and destroying all before him. The elder of the two daughters said she would go out and

drive him away.   Her mother tried to persuade her not, but she insisted, and, catching up
a rake on her way—in order to stand further
from him than her sister did—she went into
the garden and struck the bull with it.   But the
rake stuck to the bull and her hand stuck to the
rake, and off the bull started over high hills,
low hills, grey mountains, and green plains,
running without once stopping for three days
and three nights till she at length saw a great
castle the colour of blood, and here she stopped,
and the bull turned himself into a man, and
there she beheld the very prince who had gone
away from her mother's castle in wrath not
long before.

"Fair princess," said he, "you may remember
that when I quitted your mother's castle my last
words were that when I came again you would
come with me without my asking you. Haven't
I kept my word?"

Then he led her into the castle and told her
she would be mistress of it; and, if she so willed
it, might be as happy as the day was long, for
he would permit her the enjoyment of every
pleasure, and put every pleasure in her way—

only, let her beware not to disobey any of his orders else the fate of many others, whose blood now coloured the walls of his castle, would be hers.

Next morning he called her, and telling her he was going to be absent for two days, gave her the keys of all the rooms in the castle, telling her she might amuse herself looking through them, and beholding their magnificence, till he returned. But he pointed out one and warned her on her peril not to open the room of which that was the key.

The prince departed, and the young princess immediately set about going through the many magnificent rooms which the castle contained, and her amazement at their grandeur was great. She had opened and entered every room but the forbidden one, and coming to that door and examining it she began debating with herself why it was he had ordered her not to enter it, and came to the conclusion that it must contain some wonderful secret when he was so strict in excluding her from it. At length she resolved to just open it and peep in, saying that it would be impossible for the prince ever to

find out her disobedience. So she turned the key in the door, and, opening it, she saw something red on the floor, to which she put her foot and found it was blood.   Then, looking round the room, she saw the horrible sight of many bodies of beautiful ladies, and her own lost sister amongst them, hung by the walls.   She quickly closed the door and locked it.   But she found her foot was covered with blood, and when she went to the stream that flowed by the castle to wash it, though she rubbed and rubbed ever so hard, she could not get any of the blood off her foot.   Then she gave it up, saying to herself that she would manage to conceal it from her lord.

That evening as she sat under the trees in the garden eating bread and drinking milk for supper, a cat crept up to lick some drops of milk that had fallen on the ground.   She kicked away the cat.

"Miaow! Miaow!" said the cat, "if you let me take what milk drops from your bowl, I shall lick one-half the blood off your foot."

"Get out!" said she, making another kick at

the cat, "When I couldn't wash it off myself, I'm very sure you couldn't lick it off."

Then a robin redbreast hopped up to pick the crumbs she let fall; but she threw a stick at the robin and hunted it away.

"Toowhit! toowhit!" said the robin from the tree where it alighted. "If you let me pick up what crumbs fall from you I'll tell you how you may take one-half the blood off your foot."

"Get out!" said she, throwing another stick at him. "When I couldn't wash it off myself I'm very sure you couldn't tell me how."

At the end of the two days the prince returned and demanded the keys.

"I trust you haven't gone into the room I forbade you of?" he said. "Show me your feet."

She tried to hide the bloody foot from him, but it was of no use, for he insisted on seeing it; and, finding the blood upon it, he knew she had been in the secret room, and he immediately killed her, and hung up her body beside her sister's.

About a week after the second sister's disappearance, the queen and her only daughter, the youngest, sat in great grief by the window

on a morning, trying to console each
other for their great loss, when once more the
black bull appeared in the garden, rooting up
their flowers as before. The young princess
said she would go out and drive him off. Her
mother endeavoured to persuade her not to
attempt it, but she insisted, and seizing a very
long pole—in order to keep further from him
than her elder sisters—as she went she rushed
into the garden, and struck the bull with it.
But the pole stuck to the bull, and her hand
stuck to the pole; and the bull went off, and she
went off, over high hills, low hills, grey mountains, and green plains, running on and on,
without once stopping, for three days and three
nights, till at length she saw a great red castle,
painted all over with blood. Here the bull
stopped, and changed his shape into that of a
man—the very prince to whom she and her sisters had some time before refused their hands
in marriage.

"Now, fair young princess," said he, "when
you refused me and I quitted your mother's
castle, I said that the next time I went for you,

you might come without asking.   Has not my word been kept?"

Then he told her that he would make her the mistress of that great castle, and that she would want for nothing to make her happiness perfect. Only, he told her, she would have to obey him in all things; otherwise, the fate of those whose blood had painted his castle, would also be hers.

On the next morning the prince told her he was going away, to remain for three days, and he gave her a great bunch of keys which opened every room in the castle, and told her whilst he would be absent to amuse herself as best she could going through them, seeing their richness and beauty.   But he showed her one key, and told her on no account to dare enter or open the room of which that was the key.

The prince bade her good-bye and departed, and the princess, taking the great bunch of keys, went through the castle, gazing at the beauty of the many rooms in amazement and wonder, until she had seen them all but the one he had ordered her not to open.   She stood a long time before the door of this room, wondering why it was he had forbidden her to enter it

and what secret could it contain that he was so
anxious to keep from her. At length she resolved to open it and peep in anyhow, for how
should he know whether she had disobeyed him
or not. So she opened the door, and seeing
the floor covered with something red, she put
her foot to it to find what it was, and discovered
it was blood. Then she saw a very great number of bodies of beautiful ladies who had been
murdered, and hung by their long hair from
hooks round the walls. Horrified by this, she
hastily closed the door, and locked it. But she
found her foot was covered with blood, and she
went at once to the stream that flowed by the
castle for the purpose of washing it. Yet,
though she washed and washed, and scrubbed
and rubbed for hours together, she was unable
to take a single trace of blood off the foot.
Then she left. saying to herself that she would
be able to conceal it from the prince anyhow.

In the evening, as she ate her bread and
drank her milk for supper. under the trees in
the garden, a cat came creeping up to lick the
drops of milk that fell from the basin.

"Oh, poor puss!" said she, "you're thirsty

and that's not much milk for you. Here," said she, giving the half-finished basin to the creature—"Here is a drop for you, for you're thirstier than me, and I can easily do without it."

When the cat had finished the milk, "Miaow! Miaow!" it said, "put out your foot fair lady, till I lick half the blood off it."

"There it is, good cat," said she, putting it out, "but when I couldn't wash it off myself, I fear you won't be able."

But in a few moments the cat licked off half the blood. She thanked it very much and it went away, leaving her eating her bread.

Soon the robin redbreast came hopping up to pick the crumbs that fell from her.

"Poor robin," she said, "you are hungry and more in need of this bread than me, for I can easily do without it," and she laid down her bread till the robin had pecked to satisfaction of it.

"Toowhit! toowhit!" said the robin then—"I can tell you, kind lady, how to take the other half of the blood off your foot, if you do it."

"Very well, then, good robin," she said, "I'll

try.   But when I wasn't able to wash it off myself I fear you won't be able to help me."

"Pluck ten leaves of the yarrow to-night at midnight," said the robin.   "Throw the tenth away and boil the other nine.   Then wash your foot in the boiled juice and the blood will wash off."

She thanked the little robin, who flew away, and at midnight she went into the garden and plucked ten leaves of the yarrow, throwing the tenth away, and boiling the other nine.   In the juice she washed her foot, and every trace of the blood was gone.

When, at the end of the three days, the prince returned, he demanded the keys.

"I hope," said he, "you haven't disobeyed me, and opened the forbidden room.   Show me your feet."

She showed him her feet which would shame snow in whiteness.

"I see you have not disobeyed me," he said, "and I am glad, for I would not like to kill so beautiful a lady.   Your two sisters whom I took away, and many other beautiful ladies before that, when put to the test, disobeyed me, and I killed them and hung them up by the hair in that very room.   You have not disobeyed me, and I will make you my wife, for you have nothing more to fear now that I have found you are without that curiosity which is the great blemish on most women.   Here," he said, handing her a white rod, "is a wand.   Go to the secret room, open it, and going in, strike the bodies of your sisters with it."

She did this, and lo! her sisters came to life once more.   The prince then allowed her to bring to life in the same way all the other young ladies who had been killed and hung up in the room, and they were sent to their homes again.

The young princess found herself very much in love with the prince, for he was a most handsome man; and she now gladly agreed to become his wife.   Her mother was soon made acquainted with what had happened, and her joy was great at finding her beautiful daughters still alive.   She came to the marriage, as did all the other nobility; and it was allowed on all hands that a more beautiful or a happier pair had never before been united.   The marriage lasted nine days and nine nights; the last day

and night was as good as the first, and the first
as good as the last; and the handsome prince
and his beautiful princess lived happily ever
after.

The Old Hag of the Forest

THE OLD HAG OF THE FOREST

Once on a time, long long ago, when there were more kings and queens in Ireland than O'Donnell's old castle has windows, and when witches and enchantments were as plentiful as blackthorn bushes, there was a king and a queen with three sons, and to every one of these sons the queen had given a hound, a hawk and a filly. The filly could overtake anything, the hound could catch anything it pursued on dry land, and the hawk could come up with anything in the air or in the water. In the course of time, when these three lads had grown up to be fine, able, strapping young men, the oldest said one day that he would go away to push his fortune. The king and the queen were vexed at this, and wrought him high up and low down to keep him from going, but it was all no use, he wouldn't be said by them, and so, asking

127

their blessing, he mounts the filly, and, with the hawk on his shoulder, and the hound at his heels, sets out. And he told them as he was setting out, to watch, from day to day, the water that settled in the filly's hoof-tracks outside the gate, "for," says he, "as long as that water keeps clear I'm all right; but when you see it frothing, I'm fighting a hard battle; and if ever you see it turn bloody I'm either dead or under enchantment." So himself, the hound, the hawk and the filly, they started, and off with them, and they traveled away, and away, far further than I could tell you and twice further than you could tell me, till at last one evening late he comes in sight of a great castle. When he got sight of the castle he pulls up his filly, and, looking about him, he sees a small wee house convaynient and he drew on this house, and, going in, found only one old woman in it and saw that it was a neat, clean little house entirely. "God save ye, young gentleman," says the woman. "God save yerself, kindly, and thanky; and can I have lodging for the night for myself, my hound, my hawk, and my filly?" says he. "Well for yourself, you can," says the old woman, says she, "but I don't like them other animals, but sure you can house them outside," says she. Very well and good, he agreed to this. When the old woman was getting his supper for him she said she supposed he was for the big fight the morrow. He axed her, "What big fight?" "And och," says she, "is that all you know about it," commencing and telling to him how that the king's daughter of the castle beyond was to be killed by a great giant the next day unless there was a man there able to beat the giant, and to any man that would fight him and beat him the king was to give his daughter in marriage and the weight of herself three times over in goold. "Och," says he, "I'll find something better to do. I'll not go near it." So the next morning early he was up betimes and pretending he was going away to hunt; but doesn't he go instead to the king's castle, and there he saw no end of a crowd gathered together from the four winds of the world, some of them thinking to fight the giant and win the king's daughter, and more of them only come out of curiosity, just to look on. But when the

giant made his appearance, and they saw the
sight of him, not a man of all the
warriors there, covered all over as they were
in coats of iron mail from the crown of their
heads to the soles of their feet—the sorra re-
saive the one of them, but went like that, trembling with fear, for the like of such a tar-riffic
giant none of them ever saw or heerd tell of
before. So, my brave king's son waited on till
he saw there was none of them present would
venture to fight the giant, and then out he steps
himself ; and the giant and him to it, and the like
of their fight was never witnessed in Ireland before or since, and he gave the giant enough to
do, and the giant gave him enough to do ; till at
last, when it was going hard with him, he gave
one leap into the air, and coming down
with his sword just right on the giant's
neck, he cut off his head, clean off, and
then when he had that done he disappeared
in the crowd, and after killing some game
on the hills came home and gave the old
woman the game for supper. That night when
the old woman was giving him his supper she
told him about the great gentleman that had

killed the giant that day, and then disappeared
all of a suddint into the air. And then she
said that giant's brother was to be there the
morra to fight anyone that would fight for the
king's daughter, and she told him he should go,
for it would be well worth seeing. But, "Och,"
says he, "I'll find something better worth doing—I'll not go near it." So after his supper,
to bed he went, and he was up again early betimes in the morning, and making pretend he
was going to hunt, he went off to the castle
again. This day the crowd was bigger than
ever, and when the giant appeared, if the
first giant was tar-riffic, this one was twice over
double as tar-riffic, and he could get no man
with the heart to venture to fight him, till at
length my brave king's son had to step out this
day again and encounter him. Well, if the
fight was hard the first day, it was this day
double as hard, and the giant gave him his fill
of it, and he gave the giant his fill of it, till at
long and at last when it was going hard on him
he takes one spring right up into the air and
landing down with his sword on the giant's
neck he cuts the head right off from the body

and then again disappeared in the crowd, and
after a while's hunting on the hills he come
home with plenty of game; and this night, just
like the night afore, when the old woman
was giving him his supper she made great wonders of telling him of the tar-riffic fight that day
again between the strange gentleman and the
giant, and how he killed the giant and then disappeared right up into the sky before all their
eyes. And then she said that on the morra the
third and last giant was to fight, and she said
this would be a wonderful day entirely, and he
should surely go to see it, and to see the wonderful gentleman that killed the other
two giants. But "Och," says he, "I'll
find something better to do—I'll not go
near it, to look at him or it." And
the third morning again he went to the
castle, purtending that it was to hunt he was
goin', and the third giant appeared, and him far
more tar-riffic than the first two put together.
And to make a long story short, my brave
king's son and himself went at it, and the fighting was the most odious* ever was witnessed

* Odious is a very comprehensive word in the mouth
of a Donegal shanachy.   It generally means everything
inexpressible by the English language.

before or since, and the short and the long of it
was that he sprung up at length into the air,
and coming down on the giant's neck cut off his
head, and then again disappeared in the crowd
and went home; but as he was disappearing,
doesn't one of the king's men snap the shoe off
his foot; so home he had to go that night wanting one shoe.   Next day, and for eight days
after, the king had all his men out scouring the
country far and wide to see if they could find
the owner of the shoe; but though they flocked
to the castle in thousands not one of them
would the shoe fit.   And every one of these days
the king's son was out with his filly, his hawk
and his hound on the hills hunting.   At last one
day the old woman went to the castle and told
how she had a lodger that come home the night
the last giant was kilt with one boot wanting.
And the next day the king came there himself
with a carriage and four horses and took the
king's son away to his castle, and there when
they tried on him the boot, doesn't it fit him like
as if it was made on his foot; and the king gave
him his daughter, and the marriage was per-
formed, and all the whole gentry and nobility

of all the land was invited in to a big faist. But,
lo and behould ye, on that very night when all
the spree was going on, and the fun was at its
heighth in the ballroom, and all were as busy as
bees in the kitchen, what would ye have of it
but at that very ins'ant doesn't there come to
the kitchen window a hare, and puts in its
head and commences licking a plate of
some particular nice dainty that was cool-
ing inside the window, and the cook
was so enraged at one of her very best
dishes being destroyed that she got up in a
passion and put off her all sorts and said it was
a nice how do ye do that, with a hairo in the
house that had killed giants, a dirty hare would
be allowed to come in and spoil her cook-
ing. This word soon came to the groom's
ears in the ball-room, and though the king
and the queen and the bride and all the
nobility and gentry tried to persuade him
against it he wouldn't stop, and there was no
holding of him. He said he wouldn't sleep two
nights in the one bed, or eat two meals' meat
in the one house, till he would catch that
hare and bring it back dead or alive. So mount-

ing his filly, and taking with him his hawk and
his hound, he started off hot-foot in pursuit. He
pursued the hare all that night and all the next
day, and at evening late he drew on a little wee
house he saw in a hollow, and he went in, for he
was tired, and determined to rest that night. He
wasn't long in, and he was warming himself
at the fire, with his hound, his hawk and his
filly, when he hears a noise at the wee window
of the house, and there he sees a dirty wizened
old hag of a woman, trembling and shaking
down to her very finger tips. "Och, och, och,
it's cold, cold, cold," says she, and her teeth
rattling in her head. "Why don't you come in
and warm yourself?" says he. "Och, I can't, I
can't," says she. "I'm afeerd of them wild animals of yours.   But here," says she, pulling
three long hairs out of her head, and handing
them in by the window to him, "here," says
she, "is three of the *borochs** we used to have
in old times, and if you tie them wild beasts of
yours with them then I'll go in." So he took the
three hairs and tied the hawk, the hound and

---

* The *boroch* is the rope used in tying a cow to the
stake.

the filly with them, and then the old hag came in, but she was trembling no longer, and, says she, with her eyes flashing fire, "Do you know who I am?" says she. "They call me the Old Hag of the Forest, and it was my three sons you killed to win the king's daughter, but you'll pay dearly for it now," says she. With that he drew his sword, and the hag drew another, and both of them fell to it, and I couldn't be able to describe to you the terrible fight they had entirely. But at length the Old Hag of the Forest was getting too many for him, and he had to call on the help of the hound. "Hound, hound," says he, "where are you at my command?" And at this, "Hair, hair," says the old hag, says she, "hold tight." "O," says the hound, "it's hard for me to do anything and my throat a-cutting." Then he called on the hawk. "Hawk, hawk," says he, "where are you at my command?" And, "Hair, hair," says the old hag, says she, "hold tight." "O," says the hawk, "sure it's hard for me to do anything and my throat a-cutting. And then he called on the filly. "Filly, filly," says he, "where are you at my command?" "Hair, hair," says the old hag, says she, "hold tight." "O," says the filly, "sure it's hard for me to do anything and my throat a-cutting." So the end of it all was that the hag overcome him, and then taking out of her pocket a little white rod she struck him with it, and turned him into a gray rock, just outside her door, and then striking the hound, the hawk and the filly with the rod she turned them into white rocks just beside him.

Now, at home, they watched the water in the filly's hoof tracks as regular as the sun rose every day, day after day, till at last they one day saw the water in the hoof tracks frothing, and they said he was fighting a hard battle; and so he was, for that was the very day himself and the first giant had the encounter. Next day it was frothing more than ever, for that was the day he was fighting the second giant, and on the third day the water frothed right up out of the tracks, and then they knew he was fighting a desperate big battle entirely; and sure enough himself and the third giant were at it hard and fast at the same ins'ant. But at length didn't they find the water turning to blood and they thought he must be killed. So the next morn-

ing the second brother set out and he said he
wouldn't sleep two nights in the one bed nor eat
two meals of meat in the one house till he'd find
out what happened to his brother. He took his
hound, his hawk and his filly with him and he
traveled on and on, far further than I could tell
you, and twice further than you could tell me,
till at length one evening late doesn't he come to
the very wee house near a great castle where his
brother had put up before him. And when he
comes in the old woman that was in the house
flew at him and kissed him and welcomed him
back with a hundred welcomes ten times over,
for he was so like his brother she was sure it
was him was in it. Then she told him that they
were all waiting for him anxiously at the castle,
expecting him back every day, and that he
should lose no time in going to them, for that
the bride in particular was down-hearted entirely since he had went away, thinking that
she'd never see him no more. So off he starts
at once for the castle to find it all out, and it's
there was the welcome and the rejoicing, and
the pretty king's daughter covered him all over
with kisses, and there was a great spread, and

all the gentry and nobility were asked in again,
but that night again, what would you have of
it, but the hare comes a second time, and spoiled
the cook's best dish, and drove the cook into a
frightful rage, and—"It's a nice how do ye do,
indeed," says the cook, says she, "that with a
hairo in the house that slew three giants a
hare would be allowed to come in and spoil my
very choicest dish, and then go off with itself
scot free," says she. And this word come to
the new groom in the ballroom, and "By this,
and by that," says he, "I won't stop till I go
after that hare, and I'll never stop two nights or
eat two meals in the one house 'till I bring back
that hare dead or alive." And so, off he starts,
himself, the hound, the hawk, and the filly; and
all that night and the next day he purshued
after the hare, and late the next evening when
he was feeling tired out and not able to follow
any further doesn't he see in the hollow below
him a little house, and drawing on the house,
he went in and was warming himself by the fire
with his hound, his hawk and his filly about
him when he hears a noise at the window, and
there he sees an old hag quaking and shaking

all over. "Och, och, och, it's cold, cold, cold," says she, trembling all over. "Why don't you come in and warm yourself?" says he. "O," says she, "I couldn't go in, for I'm afeerd of them wild animals of yours. But here," says she, pulling three long hairs out of her head, "here's three of the kind of *borochs* we used to use long ago, and tie your animals with them, and then I'll go in." So he takes the hairs and ties the hound, the hawk and the filly with them, and then the old hag came in, and she not trembling at all now, but her eyes flashing fire, and, says she, "Your brother killed my three sons, and I made him pay dearly for it, and I'll make you pay dearly," says she, "too." So with that she drew a sword, and he drew a sword, and both of them to it, and they fought long and they fought hard, but the hag was too many for him, so at length he had to call on the hound. "Hound, hound," says he, "where are you at my command?" Says the old hag, says she, "Hair, hair, hold tight!" "O," says the hound, "how could I do anything and my throat a-cutting?" Then he called on the hawk.

"Hawk, hawk," says he, "where are you at my command?" "Hair, hair," says the old hag, says she, "hold tight!" "O," says the hawk, "how could I do anything and my throat a-cutting?" Then he called on his filly. "Filly, filly," says he, "where are you at my command?" "Hair, hair," says the old hag, says she, "hold tight!" "O," says the filly, says he, "how could I do anything and my throat a-cutting?" So the end of it all was again that the hag got the better of him, and, taking out a wee bit of white rod out of her pocket she struck him with it, and turned him into another gray stone outside the door, and then struck the hound, the hawk and the filly, and turned them into three white stones just beside him.

Now, at home as before, they were watching his filly's hoof tracks every day regular, and everything went well till at last one day they saw the water in them turn bloody and then they were afeerd he was kilt. Then the very next morning says the youngest son Jack, says he, "I'll start off with my hound, my hawk and my filly, and won't sleep two nights in one

bed, or eat two meals in the one house till I
find what has happened to my two older brothers." So off he starts—himself, his filly, his
hawk, and his hound—and he traveled and
traveled away, far further than you could tell
me or I could tell you, till he come in sight of
the very same castle his two brothers reached
before him, and drawing on the wee hut he saw
near it he went in, and the old woman jumped
and threw her arms about his neck, and welcomed him home with a hundred thousand welcomes, and told him it was a poor thing to go
away and leave his bride the way he did, twice,
and that she was in a very bad way, down-
hearted entirely, thinking and ruminating what
had become of him, or happened to him at all,
at all. And then she hurried my brave Jack off
to the castle. And, och, it's there the welcome
was for him and the rejoicements, bekase he
had come back again. And this time, just as before, the great faist was given, and the gentry
and nobility all asked in to it, and the play was
at its heighth when the word come to the ball-
room once more about the unmannerly hare
spoiling the cook's best dish the third time, and

how the cook said it was a purty how de ye do,
entirely, that such a thing would be allowed,
with a hairo in the house that slew three giants.
And with that, without more ado, off my brave
Jack insisted on starting, and there was no
holding of him, good or bad, for he said he
was bound to fetch back that hare, dead
or alive. So off Jack starts himself, his
hawk, his hound and his filly, and Jack
had a sort of notion in his eye that
this same hare was nothing good, and that
'twas it led his two brothers astray, whatever
had happened to them. So he traveled on, and
on, and on, for that night and all the next day,
and never come up with the hare, till at length,
late that evening, he saw from him the same
wee hut in the hollow that his brothers drew on
before, and on it my brave Jack drew, too. And
after he had been in the cabin some time himself, his hound, his hawk and his filly, he hears
the noise at the window, and there he sees the
old hag, trembling and shaking and quaking,
and "Och, och, och, but it's cold, cold, cold,"
says she: "And why." says he, "don't you come
in and warm yourself?" "Och," says she, "I'm

afeerd of them wild animals of yours. But
here," says she, taking out of her head three
hairs, "here's three of the kind of *borochs* we
used to use in old times, and tie your animals
with them, and then I'll go in." Jack took from
her the three hairs, and, pretending to tie the
hound, the hawk and the filly with them, he
threw them instead into the fire. Then the old
hag came in, her eyes blazing in her head, and,
drawing a sword, she rushes at Jack to have his
life. And Jack drew his sword and rushed at
her, and both of them to it hard and fast, and
they fought long and they fought hard, till at
length Jack, finding the hag putting too sore on
him, called on his hound. "Hound, hound,
where are you at my command?" "Hair, hair,"
says the old hag, says she, "hold tight!" "O,"
says the hair, "it's hard for me to do good and
me a-burning in the fire." And then Jack called
on his hawk. "Hawk, hawk," says he, "where
are you at my command?" "Hair, hair," says
the old hag, says she, "hold tight." "O," says
the hair, "it's hard for me to do good and me
a-burning in the fire." Then Jack called on his
filly. "Filly, filly," says he, "where are you at

my command?" "Hair, hair," says the old hag,
says she, "hold tight." "O," says the hair,
"it's hard for me to do good and me a-burning
in the fire." So the hound, the hawk and the filly
all rallied to my brave Jack's aid, and the hound
got hold of the hag by the heel and wouldn't
let her go all she could do; and with one fling
the filly broke her leg, and the hawk picked out
her two eyes, so she couldn't see what she was
doing, or where she was striking. So then, she
cried out, "Mercy, mercy, spare my life and I'll
give you back your two brothers." "All right,"
says Jack, "tell me where they are, and how I'm
to get them." "Do you see them two gray
stones," says she, "outside the door, with three
smaller white ones round each of them?" "I
do," says Jack. "Well," says she, "the gray
stones are your brothers, and the others are
their hounds, their hawks, and their fillies; and
if you take water from the well at the foot of
that tree below the house, and sprinkle three
drops of it on each of them stones, they'll all be
disenchanted again." Jack, you may suppose,
didn't lose much time doing this, and lo and behold you from the stones comes up his two

brothers, every one of them with his hound,
his hawk, and his filly, just the same as they
were before they had been enchanted by the old
Hag of the Forest, and that was the meeting
and the greeting between Jack and his lost
brothers, that he thought he'd never see again!
But off they soon started, all of them, with their
hounds, their hawks and their fillies, away
back for the castle again, and the eldest brother
got his bride and the faist was spread this time
again and all the gentry and nobility of both
that and the surrounding countries all come to
attend it and do honor to the bride and groom;
and such a time for eating, drinking, dancing,
singing, fun and amusement was never seen before or after. Jack and the second brother
started away off afterwards for home with their
hounds, their hawks and their fillies with them
and as much goold as they could carry. I got
brogues of *brochan** and slippers of bread, a
piece of a pie for telling a lie, and then come
slithering home on my head.

* Porridge.

Rory the Robber

RORY THE ROBBER

RORY was the greatest robber in that whole country, and there was a great gentleman lived there who owned a great estate in a distant part of the country. But he never got any good of the estate, for whoever he sent to lift the rents was always sure to be robbed by Rory in the mountains coming home again, and maybe killed into the bargain. So the gentleman found it was no use trying to lift the rents, and for the past five years he gave up lifting them altogether. Then there was a boy named Billy come to the gentleman looking to be hired, and the gentleman axed what he could do; and Billy said he could do anything, and then the gentleman engaged him. And when that time of year came, says Billy, says he, to his masther, "Masther," says he, "are ye sendin' no one to lift your rents this year?" "No, Billy," says the masther, "for it is no use. Rory would only rob them, and maybe murder them into the bargain on the way back." Says Billy, says he, "I'll try." Well and good the masther consinted, and told Billy to harness the best horse in the stable, so that he might have a chance of escaping from Rory. "No," says Billy, "but give me the very worst horse." And the worst horse Billy saddled, and went off. And when he was going through the mountains he enquired for Rory, and finding him out, he told him, says he, "I'm Billy, the masther's boy, and I'm going to such a place" (mentioning the name of where the estate was), says he, "to collect his rents; and if you're here when I'm coming back, I'll hand the money over to you." Rory thanked him for nothing, and said he would be there right enough to take the rents from him. So, when Billy got to the estate and collected the rents in gold and notes, he had it all sewed into the lining of his coat, all except ten pounds that he changed into coppers and tied up in a bag, and put on the saddle before him. And when he reached the mountains on his way back, there he met Rory waiting for him. Then, says Billy, "I want to purtend to

my masther that I made a hard fight before I
gev up the money, so do you," says he, holding
out his coat, "shoot your pistols through that
coat, that I can be able to show him the marks."
Then Rory shot all his pistols through Billy's
coat, making a number of holes in it.   Then
Billy threw the bag of coppers on the road, and
says he, "There's the rints," and when Rory
got down off his horse to lift the bag, Billy
jumped up on it, and away off, and it was one
of the swiftest horses in the country, so that
Rory couldn't overtake him, and he couldn't
fire after him, because Billy was so cute as to
make him empty all his pistols into his coat.

When Billy got home to his masther, and gev
him up the rints, and told him the whole story
of how he had tricked Rory, his masther was
proud of him, and couldn't make too much of
him.   "But then," says the masther, "it was a
bad thing to take his horse, for he'll never rest
contented now till he's revenged on me." They
agreed it was best to leave back the horse with
Rory, and so Billy started, and when he fell
in with the robber and gev him up his horse,
Rory said he was a clever fellow and no mis-

take, and he would like Billy would join his band. Billy said well and good, he would. Off they went, then, to the cave in the mountains where the robbers had their den, and when they came there Rory introduced Billy to his brother robbers, and they proposed to welcome him with a big supper.   So one of their clever-est hands was sent away to steal a sheep that they might make a fine roast.   He was a long time away and they begun to chat about what was keeping him. "I'll bet you fifty pounds," says Billy to Rory, "that I steal the sheep from him." "Done," says Rory. Then Billy started away, and taking off a pair of splendid big top boots he had on him, he dropped one of them about a mile from the cave in the path the robber would take coming home with the sheep, and then travelling on about half a mile further he dropped the other, after rubbing it well with soft mud to make it right dirty.   Then, when, not long afther, the robber comes along with the sheep, and comes up to this boot, he looks at it and says "It's a fine top-boot, but, bad luck to it," says he, "it's too dirty entirely to carry, and where's the use of it anyhow when I haven't its

fellow?" On he went then himself and
the sheep till he come to the next boot,
and when he seen it "Bad scran to me,"
says he, "but there is its fellow, and I
was unlucky I didn't take it." So he took
and tied the sheep to a stump of a bush that was
bye, and started away back to get the other top-
boot. In the meantime Billy loosed the sheep
and took it to the cave, and got his bet from
Rory. Soon the robber come then to the cave
with the pair of top-boots in his hand, and told
how he tied the sheep to the stump of a bush till
he'd go back and look for the other top-boot, and
how, when he come back, the sheep was broke
away, and he couldn't get her. Then Rory
ordered him to go back and steal another sheep;
"And now," says he to Billy, when he was gone,
"I'll hold ye a hundred pound ye don't steal this
sheep from him." "Done," says Billy, and
started off after him. When Billy got to the
place he had stole the first sheep he hid close by,
and waited till the robber come up with the
next; and when he come up Billy commenced
bleatin' like a sheep and "Bad luck be off me,"
says the robber, says he, "but there's the sheep I

lost." And with that he tied the sheep he had with him now to the very same tree stump, and went over the ditches looking for the other sheep. Billy stole round, and loosed the sheep, and away to the cave with it, and won that hundred pounds too.

Rory had to confess that Billy was by far the cleverest thief he ever met, and even cleverer than himself. "I'll tell you what," says he to Billy, "there's one thing I want stolen, and I have been after it for the last five years and couldn't succeed—but maybe you'd come better speed than me; it's the King of Connaught's black mare, the grandest and swiftest in the world, that never was beaten yet, or never will be beaten; if I only had her, I would defy the whole country, for none could catch me. I'll give you, Billy," says he, "four hundred pounds in goold if ye can succeed in stealing her for me. But it's a very difficult job," says he, "for there's always a guard of soldiers on the stable, and a man sitting on the back of the black mare, night and day, for fear of me stealing her." "Well," says Billy, "if I had only a good harper

to come with me I'd steal her." "Well," says
Rory, "you have that here, for I'm reckoned
a first-class player on the harp, and my father
before me was harper to the Chieftain of
Knockree." Well and good, then, Billy made
him disguise as a blind harper, and they both of
them set off, and the harp with them, for the
King of Connaught's castle, and Billy put
Rory to play the harp before the castle windows where there was a lot of high-up folk being entertained. And when the King of Connaught saw the blind harper he made him be
brought in to amuse the company, and then, of
course, a dance was started, and every one was
taken up with the fun, the captain of the guards
along with every one else. Then, when Billy
found the spree at its height, he went and got a
jar of whiskey and drugged it with sleeping
drops, and then went into the courtyard and lay
down close by the stables, like a drunken man
fallen asleep, with the drugged jar beside him.
The guards soon saw the jar, and smelled it,
and saying to themselves that there was no
watch over them this night, when everybody
was too taken on with the fun, and that it

would be no harm to taste just a little of it, they passed the jar round, and
every man of them fell fast asleep; and
the man that was on the horse's back
dropped off it, asleep with the drink, too;
and Billy got up and went into the stable, and
taking out the black mare, started off with her
to the mountains. And when Rory arrived
he was a proud man to find the King of Connaught's black mare there before him. He
counted down to Billy four hundred yellow,
shining sovereigns, and Billy went home with
his five hundred and fifty pounds, and lived an
honest and happy man ever after.

Myles McGarry and Donal
McGarry

MYLES McGARRY AND DONAL McGARRY

ONCE on a time there was two brothers, Myles McGarry and Donal McGarry, and they had only a *weeshy* wee bit of a sod of land that they called a farm, but it was that small that a daicent crow with any self-respect would be ashamed to live on it; and, though Myles and Donal was two hard workin', industhrus boys close on to forty-five years of age, and worked early and late, in fair weather and foul, the dickens a bit of them could make as much out of the wee sparrow park as would keep body and sowl together, so sez Myles to Donal, sez he, one mornin' in the latther end o' harwust, sez he: "Now, Donal, asthore, as we've got in the wee crop safe and sound, and there's nothing more to do again' the winther, it wouldn't hould me," sez Myles, sez he, "to sthart away and hire till the Wareday comes round again,

159

when I'll maybe find something to do helping you to put in a wee bit of crop. In the mane-time, keep you a tight grip on the farm and don't let it blow away when the wind rises." So, spitting on his staff, and wishing Donal "God prosper him," off he stharted, and away he travelled afore him for long an' long, till at length he come into a strange country, where he fell in with a gentleman-looking man; and this lad asked him where was he going, or what was a trouble to him.

"I'm looking for a masther," sez Myles.

"Well, by the powdhers," sez the gentleman-looking man, sez he, "but I'm looking for a sarvant."

"Well and good," sez Myles, sez he, "I think we could do worse nor strike up. What's your tarms?" sez Myles.

"Well, my tarms," sez the gentleman-looking man, "my tarms," sez he, "is a wee bit out of the ornery. The pay," sez he, "is purty good; I'll give fifty pounds for a good sarvant, from now till the cuckoo has called three times—only this: any boy hires with me must never confess himself out of timper, or displaised

with me; at the same time that I'll agree never
to confess myself out of timper or displaised
with him; and if aither of us breaks this un-
dherstanding he's to allow his two ears to be
clipped off with the woolshears by the other.
Do you consint to them tarms?" sez he.

"Well," sez Myles, sez he, "the tarms is what
I call a bit quare; but, stillandever, considher-
ing that I favour the look of ye—and I think
your'e a jintleman—and as I know that I have
a fairishly good timper meself, and as the wages
is nate—why, I say all things considered, I'm
inclined to be of opinion that I might go further
and fare worse. So considher me hired."

Very good, Myles went home with his masther and had nothing to do that night, but got a
good supper, and went to his bed, and in the
morning when he got up the masther was with
him immediately and sez :—

"Go out," sez he, "to the barn, and start
thrashin' that wee grain of corn. There's not
much in it," sez he, "and ye'll not get your
breakwist till you have done."

Well and good. Off Myles started, whistling, to the barn. But when he got there and

looked in of the door, my faix, his tune **was**
soon changed, for there was as good as six ton
of corn piled and panged up to the roof.

"Phew-ew-ew!" sez Myles, "there's some
mistake here, surely. There's siveral days'
thrashin' of corn there, and he can't expect one
to have that done by breakwist time. . But I'll
do what I can, anyhow, and thrash away till
they call me in."

But Myles, unfortunate christian that he
was, he thrashed and thrashed away, and if he'd
been thrashin' since there wouldn't one of them
have come out to call him in to his breakwist.
So my poor Myles thrashed away, and pegged away, till he had a heap of corn as big as
a wee hill, and a pile of straw as big as a mountain before and behind him, and by that time it
was falling night, and no one having come to
call him, he pitched the flail from him as far as
he could throw it and pushed for the house.
There he met the masther.

"Well, Myles," sez the masther, "it can't be
that it's only now ye're finishin' that wee grain
of corn?" sez he.

"Finishin' it!" sez Myles, scornfully, that

way after him—"Finishin' it, in troth! No, nor it's not well begun. Nice thrashers," sez he, "ye must have in this part of the country if they do the like of that afore breakwist."

"Oh!" sez the masther, "so it's what ye haven't done yet, then? Very well, ye get no breakfast till it's finished—but I won't refuse you sleep. You can go to bed for the night, and go at it fresh in the morning."

Myles listened to him for a while, and then he flew out in a passion.

"And is that the way ye're goin' to thrate me, a daicent woman's son, to send me to bed breakwistless, dinnerless, and supperless, and go out to thrash the morra mornin' again fresh and fastin' on the bare-footed stomach—is that the way, ye onnatural brute, ye, is that the way—"

"Aisy, aisy," sez the masther. "Are ye angry with me, Myles?"

Then Myles minded his bargain, and he got down in the mouth, and,

"Oh, no, no," sez he, "I'm not angry with ye at all, at all."

And with that he went to his bed, and next

morning he was up and out early to his **work**, and there the poor fellow worked and sweated, and thrashed and thrashed, till he was fairly falling down with the hunger and waikness, and he seen that at this rate it's dead he'd be afore he got half through with the corn.   And at this time, who looks in of the barn door with a snicker of a laugh in his throat but the masther.

"Well, Myles," sez he, "not breakwist **time** yet I see?"

This was too much for flesh and blood **to** stand.   He draws the flail one polthogue at the lad in the door, and just barely missed him **by** a hair's breadth.

"What, Myles, Myles," sez he, "sure it's **not** angry with me you are?"

"Is it not, though?" sez Myles, "I wish," sez he, "the ould divel had ye, for ye're the most onnatural brute I ever come across,—bad **scran** to ye!"

"All right, all right," sez he, "down on **your** knees with ye," and taking hold of the wool-shears he left poor Myles' head in a couple of minutes as bare of ears as the head of a herrin'. And off poor Myles started for home, and reached Donal and the farm in a woful plight. And he starts and rehearses to Donal the whole norration of all happened to him.

"Never mind," sez Donal, sez he, when he finished—"Never mind," sez he, "if I don't get even with him. Just you stop at home, now, Myles," sez he, "and keep the farm from blowing away, till I go and see how him and me can agree."

So spitting on his stick, and in the same way, wishing Myles, "God prosper him," he started off, and travelled away afore him for days and nights till he come to the same strange country and fell in with the very same man that Myles did. And the man said he was looking for a good sarvant, and Donal said he was looking for a good masther; so the long and the short of it was that Donal engaged on the very same tarms Myles did.

The very next morning after he hired, the masther tould him to go out and thrash a wee grain of corn was in the barn afore he'd get his breakwist. Donal went out and started the thrashing, and the first cart he saw passin' the

way going to the next town, he gathered up a
bag of the corn and threw it on it, telling the
driver to sell it in the town and fetch him back
the worth of it in provisions, aitables and so-
forth.   Faix, my brave Donal thrashed away
at his aise for three or four days whistlin' like a
thrush, and aitin' and drinkin' like a lord, and
every day regular the ould tyrant would come
and look in, and ax him how he was getting
along.   "As snug as a bug in a rug," me brave
Donal would tell him, and then whistle up a
livelier jig, and the ould fella would go away
with himself, with a face as long as an under-
taker's when trade's dull, wondherin' how on
earth the lad could thrash so long without a
pick of breakwist, till at last he began to get a
bit misdoubtful of himself; and so, the fifth
day, when he gleeked in, and found Donal, if
anything, in bigger heart than usual.

"Do ye hear me, my man?" sez he to Donal.

"Oh, I'm listenin'," sez Donal, going on with
his whistling.

"Ye wouldn't be feeling hungry for a pick of
something to eat?" sez he.

"Throgs, no; I'm thankful to you," sez Donal.

He studied on himself a while, and shook his head.   "You're here, now—let me see— One, two, three, four, five—this is your fifth day," sez he, "you're here, now, and what's strikin' me as odd, bite or sup didn't cross your lips since ye come here," sez he.

"Didn't they, though?" sez Donal, back again to him that way, with a knowing wink.

This give him a sort of a start.   "And sure they didn't?" sez he.

"That's all you know about it, me rare ould buck," sez Donal, sez he, "I'm livin' like a prence," sez he, "on the best of everything, lavings and lashings, and no thanks to nobody," sez Donal.

"Livin' like a prence?" sez the ould fella. "An' in the name of powdher," sez he, "where did you get the mait?"

"I got it in the town," sez Donal, "where any one will get it that gives value for it.   There's no day the sun rises that there doesn't pass by the barn door here, goin' to the town, a string of carts as long as the day an' the morra; an' what's aisier done nor throwin' a sack of that whait on them—an' throth," sez Donal, handlin' a couple of grains of it, "bully whait it is; the shop-keepers is sendin' me out word to send in all I can of it, and they'll insure me the top of the market—what's aisier, I say," sez Donal, sez he, "than hoistin' a sack or two of that fine whait on one of them carts betimes, an' gettin' back the worth of it in the best of everything, aitable, or drinkable?" sez Donal.

"What? my whait!" sez the curmudgeon, dancing with rage.   "Is it my whait! Is it send my whait to the town, ye villainous scoundrelly——"

"Aisy, aisy, masther," sez Donal.   "Aisy, avic, *are ye displaised with me?*" sez he, that way.

Ah, an' by the boots the ould fellow didn't know whether it was on his head or his heels he was, when he seen he was cornered.   He changed the tune all at wanst.

"Oh, no, no," sez he, "I'm right well plaised with ye, Donal."

"I'm glad to hear it," sez Donal.

"Maybe *you're* displaised a bit with *me*," sez
he to Donal, thinkin' to corner him.

"Not by no mains," sez Donal. "Ye're a
bully masther, so ye are."

Well, that fared well, and the ould fellow
wint away chokin' with rage, an' plottin' an'
plannin, what anondher the sun he'd do to catch
Donal. Me brave Donal come whistlin' home
and wint to his bed, an' the nixt mornin' when
he got up, his masther comes to him, and he
give him two wild horses, and sends him out to
plough with them, and—

"Donal," sez he pointin' out the field he was
to go ploughin' in, "Donal," sez he "ye're not to
leave that bit of a field till ye have it ploughed.

"Well, masther," sez Donal, sez he, "I'll do
me best, and off Donal starts with the horses to
the field, but, phew! if Donal was workin' at
them horses from that time till now could he get
them to pull in the plough. Donal soon seen
that there was no use workin' with them so
down he sits him on the ditch, and started up
a lively lilt for company till he sees, comin'
along the road, a hawker with two miserable
old rickles of skin and bones that went undher

the name of horses—they were broken kneed,
and broken-winded, and broken-boned and
broken in everything only the appetite, and their
hides was as white with stress of age as the top
of Croagh Gorm on a Christmas mornin', and
one of them had only three legs dhrawin' pay,
and the other of them had a cough and a spit,
and together they were like a walking in-
firm'ry, and when the hawker dhrew them up
opposite where Donal was ploughin', and let
them lean up again' each other to rest, sez
Donal, sez he:

"Them's very manageable little bastes of
yours," sez he.

"Well, sure enough, I can't complain of their
being wild that way," sez the hawker.

"What do you think if you had these two fine
black horses of mine?" sez Donal.

"I'd be afther not knowin' meself with
pride if I had them spirited animals," sez he.
"Quiet bastes like this pair of mine," sez he, "is
all very well in their way; but when they come
to be so very shy and backward that ye must
pull them down wan hill, an' push them up the

next, that's what I call," sez he, "too much of a
good thing."

"Right ye are, me good man," sez Donal.
"An if ye have ten poun' on ye, I'll take that of
boot an' swap with ye."

"Done," sez the hawker.

An' then an' there both of them unloosed
their yokes an' Donal got the ten poun', an'
then tackling the two objects that it was a
moral to see, into the plough, he started work at
once, an' when his master comes out in the middle of the day to see how Donal was gettin' on
an' seen the two morals that he was sthrivin' to
drive afore him in the plough, it was hard to
say whether it was his eyes or his mouth that
he opened widest.

"I say me good man," sez he.

"Say away," sez Donal, layin' on the bastes
as hard as he could.

"Where's my two horses, I give ye this
mornin'?"

"Make use of yer eyes," sez Donal, sez he,
"an' ye'll see them."

"Get out, ye scoundhril," sez he, "them

white scarecrows aren't mine. My horses were black," sez he.

"Thrue for ye, masther," sez Donal, "so they were black this morning; but they were so uncommon hard to manage that I have coloured them white since with the sweat I tuk out iv them."

"To the dickens with that for a story," sez the ould fellow, sez he, jumpin' at Donal's throat. "Get me my horses, ye ruffian ye, or be this an' be that," sez he, "I'll not leave a bone in yer body I won't make into jelly, ye morodin' thief ye!" sez he.

"What, what, masther," sez Donal, sez he, *"sure it's not angry with me ye are?"*

"Oh, no, no, not at all," sez he, comin' to his senses at wanst—"not at all," sez he, "ye're the best boy ever I had."

"An throgs, an'," sez Donal, sez he, *"you're* the best masther iver *I* had."

An' away the masther goes with his mouth in a puss, an' away goes Donal with his tongue in his check, an' got his breakwist, an' did as he liked the remainder of that day.

Well, there the masther was in a purty

pickle, an' he didn't know, ondher the shinin' sun what to do with Donal, an' he said to himself if he had him much longer Donal would have him dead, desthroyed, ruinated entirely, an' robbed, so he took it into his head that the best thing to be done was to ordher Donal to go to the woods an' catch the wild loy-on (lion) that was killin' an' desthroyin' all afore him, an' bring him alive to his masther's house. "An' if that doesn't settle him," sez the masther, sez he, to himself, "I don't know what will."

So, gettin' up betimes next mornin', he calls Donal in.

"Donal," sez he, "there's a wild loy-on in the woods beyant, an' he's murderin' an' killin' all afore him, an' I want you go and catch him, an' lead him up here alive afore twelve o'clock this day, or if ye fail to do that I'll have ye beheaded as soon as ye come back."

"All right," sez Donal, sez he, "there's no use biddin' the divil 'good-morra' 'till ye meet him, so in the meantime I'll go and sthrive to fetch in the loy-on, an' we'll talk of the beheadin' business later."

Off for the woods then Donal starts, an' when

he got there, down on the stump of a tree me
brave Donal sits, with his considherin' cap
like, on him, an' "Donal, me lad," sez he to
himself, "ye had a good many pulls in ye, but
ye're at the en' o' yer tether now; when yerself,
me boy, an' the wild loy-on meets that will be
the last pull, an' then, och, och! the Lord be
good to poor Myles, the poor boy at home,
without a lug on him," sez he, "och, the Good-
man, pity him, what's to become of him when
I'm gone?"

All at wanst Donal sees a little red man
comin' forrid to him with a bridle in his hand.

"Ye have a wee throuble on yer heart?" sez
the wee red man, sez he, when he come forrid.

"No lie for ye," sez Donal, "I have."

"I know it all," sez the wee red man, "an'
cheer up, for I'll pull ye through."

"Is it you?" sez Donal, sez he, lookin' up and
down the wee heighth of him with a comical
look; for disthressed an' all as he was, he
couldn't help smilin' to himself at the consait
of him. "Is it you to pull me through?" sez
Donal, sez he.

"Oh, never mind," sez the wee red man,

"there's people isn't to be judged by their size,"
sez he, "I'm under obligations to your family,"
sez he, "an' I'll do you a good turn now. Take
that bridle, an' when ye meet the loy-on," sez
he, "shake it at him, and he'll be as meek as a
mouse till ye put it on him an' lead him where
ye like. But take that auger, too," sez he, "and
when ye've caught the loy-on, bore a hole in
the biggest tree in the wood, run the loy-on's
tail through the hole an' knot it on the other
side. Start him off then for the house," sez he,
an' he reached the bridle an' the auger to Donal.

Donal was all dumbfoundhered seein' he'd
made light of the little red man, for he now
saw, sure enough, he belonged to the Good People, that no man should spake or say ill of in
their hearin'. But off he starts, with the bridle
an' the auger, an' a light heart, an' he soon fell
in with the wild loy-on that was comin' on hot-
foot, roarin' an' rampagin', to devore Donal.

"It's hungry ye are for a toothful," sez
Donal, sez he, "an' maybe it's not just doin' the daicent thing to disappoint ye," sez he.
"But," sez he, shakin' the bridle at him, "there's
a time an' place for everythin' but cuttin'

corns; an' you'll get feedin' enough if ye
only hould on till I fetch ye up to my masther
an' his ould mother," sez he.

An', sure enough, the vartue was in the
bridle, for the minnit Donal shuk it at him the
loy-on give over his rampagin', an' let Donal
slip the bridle on him.

"This way, now, yer worship," sez Donal, sez
he, leadin' him to the biggest tree in the wood,
where he bored a hole with the auger an'
knotted the loy-on's tail through it, an' then
touchin' him up, started off for the house. An'
the loy-on dragged up the big tree, an' ten
acres of land that stuck to the roots of it, an'
off to the house.

But, that was the play, when Donal come
throttin' up to the house, drivin' the wild loy-on
with the tree and ten acres of land to his tail,
afore him, an' whistlin' like vingeance, "Whin
Johnny comes marchin' home!" Och-och, but
the ould boy his masther was in the devil's own
quandarry, whin Donal pulled up the devorin'
brute and the luggage behind, right at his hall-
doore, same as you might pull up an ass an' cart
an'—

"Gwoh, Johnnie," sez Donal, sez he, to the loy-on.

But, me sowl! the masther didn't wait to say, "It's thankful I am," or "'Tis well ye done it," or any other little civility of the sort but slammin' out the hall-door an' barrin', boltin', an' double-lockin' it, gallops away, an' away up the stairs to the top o' the house, an' lookin' out of the garret windy.

"Hilloa, Donal," sez he.

"I'm lindin' ye my attintion as hard as I can," sez Donal.

"Clear off out o' that, ye scoundhril ye—yerself an' that brute baste. A nice article, that," sez he, "to fetch to a man's hall-doore."

"Well, whither he's purty or not," sez Donal, sez he, "he's as God left him—an' that's a quistion by itself. But as for takin' him away, the bargain was, I was to fetch him here; but ye forgot to put in a coddy-stool* that I was to fetch him back; so, he's here now; an' here, with the help of the Lord, he'll remain, for, so far as I'm consarned, the sight of him at the hall-doore doesn't disturb me in the laste little

---

* Donal meant "the codicil."

bit, an' he may sit on his hunkers there till they make a guager of him, for all I care. In throgs, maybe I had my own throuble gettin' round the same buck—puttin' the comether on him first, an' the bridle afther, an' maybe, too, afther I had the bridle on him, an' all—maybe it would be a bit pleasanter job to ate one's breakwist than to fetch the same lad home," sez Donal, sez he.

"Oh, but Donal, ye know, Donal," sez the masther, "sure there'll be no livin' in the counthry at all, at all, with him, if he's goin' to make his sait there at my hall-doore," sez he.

"Well, there ye are now, masther," sez Donal, sez he, "an' there's the loy-on, an' between yerself an' him be it. Maybe," sez he, "if ye comed down an' had a *collogue* with him, ye might be able to raison him over, an' he might see his way to get up an' go off, himself and his applecart, back to the woods again," sez he, "won't ye come down, an' misure logic with him?" sez Donal.

"Well, troth, an' I'll not Donal," sez the masther, sez he. "thry anything o' the sort. I don't fancy at all, at all, the sort of logic that's in that lad's eye. But do you, Donal avic, like the good, daicent, obligin' boy ye always were —do you take and thurn his head right roun' and laive him back in the same place ye tuk him from, an' I'll not aisy forget it to ye; an' moreover nor that," sez he, "I'll niver, niver more, Donal, ax ye to do anything hard or conthrairy again," sez he.

"Phew! not if I know it," sez Donal. "It's the dickens's own throuble he give me to fetch him here, an' as I'm no-wise covetious of honours I'll give some other man," sez he, "the privilege of laivin' him back."

"Donal," sez the masther, sez he, "how many poun' over an' above yer wages will ye take, an' laive him the spot ye fetched him from?"

"Well, masther," sez Donal, "like Terry Hanney's pig, thon (yon) time—not puttin' the Christian in comparishment with the pig—ye have raison with ye now. Over an' above me wages, considherin' the mortial troublesome job I'm goin' to give meself," sez Donal, "I'll have no objection in the world to takin' fifty poun'," sez he, "an' laive the loy-on the spot I fetched him from."

"Donal," sez the masther, "ye couldn't do it aisier."

"Oh, the ding a aisier I could do it," sez he. "As you think it can be done chaiper, there he is, an' just say yer prayers, an' square up yer wee accounts betwixt yerself an yer sowl, an' then come down an' start in on him."

"Oh, for the sake of all the powers ever was cray-ated," sez the masther, "don't laive go of him for yer life an' sowl. Ye'll have the fifty pounds," sez he, "with a heart an' a half; only laive him back where I'll nivir see a sight o' him more," sez he.

"Me jew'l, are ye," sez Donal, sez he, touchin' up the wild loy-on, "I'll soon rid ye o' the menagerie;" an' in a jiffy he was off, himself an' the loy-on, an' the wee farm at their tail an' me brave Donal niver halted till he left back the loy-on at the very identical spot he caught him, an' onloosin' his tail an' takin' the bridle off o' him, he let him go, an' the wee red man then an' there appaired, an' Donal handed over the bridle to him, an' thanked him from his heart, an' the both o' them parted.

Afther all this was over, the ould masther

had a great consultation entirely with his ould
mother as regards what they'd do with Donal,
or how they were to get him away at all, at all,
for the Ould Fella in the Lower Counthry could
be no match for Donal; that he was a scoundhril, a rogue, an' a robber, an' that if they had
him much longer they wouldn't maybe be able
to call the very noses on their faces their own;
an' by the time the cuckoo'd call, it's in their
cowld graves they'd be when they'd hear it. So
they made up a plan that the very nixt night
they'd have a regular spree an' jollification, an'
invite in a wheen o' the naybours an' make
Donal right hearty; and in the middle of it the
ould mother would go out an' go up into the
bush outside the house an' call "Cuckoo!
cuckoo! cuckoo!" three times, an' when Donal
would hear this—seein' he'd have the dhrop in
—he wouldn't know the differ, but what it was
the rale cuckoo that was callin', an' so they'd
make him pack up an' go in the mornin'.

This was a gran' plan entirely; so the very
nixt night they had a great spree, an' the naybours was axed in, an' "Donal," sez the masther, sez he, "we'll be makin' nowise odd o'

you;ye have shown yerself a good, industhrous, obligatin' boy, that only for ye I don't know what we'd have done at all, at all," sez he, "so ye'll just dhrop in an' enjoy the night," sez he, "like any other; for we'd like to show ye whatever wee kindness we could—meself an' me poor ould mother," sez he.

Donal thanked himself an' his ould mother, an' sayed he'd surely take advantage of their very nice, kindly invitation. So Donal was at the spree, an' they put no stint of good sthrong whiskey in his way till they made him purty hearty; an' then, the masther, to show his pride in Donal—if it was thrue to him—sez:

"Donal," sez he, "could ye obligate the company by givin' us a good ould Irish song—one of the rale ould sort?" sez he.

"*Lora haincy*, I can that," sez Donal, "give them one of the rale ould style," sez he, an' he stharted up "Túirnne Mhairé," or "Mary's Wheel," with a roll that fairly put the company on their heads with delight, they niver havin' heard an Irish song afore. When he was finished, an' his masther had talked all sorts of applause to him, he commenced workin' round

· to prepare him for the cuckoo, the ould mother havin' gone out in the manetime to get up the bush—an' faix, a purty jinny-wran she was, an'—

"Donal," sez he, "it's wearin' round torst the time of year we'd be partin' now, an' I'm very sorry for it; for, throgs, though I didn't make no great bones about it, I had an oncommon great regard for ye, an' it's I'll be the sorry man when ye go."

"Faix then, masther," sez Donal, sez he, "I'll have the same story to tell meself. But I don't care if I engage with ye another tarm, at the same bargain," sez he.

"Oh, no, no, Donal," sez he, "that would niver do at all, at all; me mother an' me isn't just as well off in the world as we used to be, an' I think we'll have to give up keepin' a boy."

"Oh, anyhows, cheer up," sez Donal, sez he, "it's a far cry yet till the cuckoo calls. It's but young in the year ye know."

"Oh, ay, but Donal, ye know, this is an airly saison, entirely, an' I wouldn't be at all mismoved if I'd hear the cuckoo, now, any minute. An', more by the same token," sez he, "if I wasn't very much deludhered, it was about the shape an' size of a cuckoo I obsarved back an' forrid in the bushes aback o' the house this very evenin'," sez he.

"Well, by the patch on my breeches," sez Donal, sez he, "an' that's a fairly sizeable oath, if it was a cuckoo ye saw, an' if she thries to give us any o' her lingo in this naybourhood for a good seven weeks to come yet, she'll be afther wishin' her mother was dead-born, when I have finished with her," sez he.

But, patience saize me, if the words was well out of his mouth, when "Cuckoo! Cuckoo! Cuckoo!" was called three siviral times from the bush at the end o' the house, an' the masther looked at Donal, an' Donal raiched for the loaded gun that was standin' in a corner; an' afore one o' the company could say "Do, Donal," or "Don't, Donal," he was out through the window, an' up with the gun to his shouldher, an' lets bang at the bush the cuckoo—if it was thrue for her—called from, an' down tumbles his masther's ould mother, head foremost, out of the tree, as dead as a salted herrin'.

An', och, there was then the *roolie-boolie.*

"Och, ye tarnation black-hearted rascal ye," sez the masther, sez he, "ye have done it at last, ye have done it at last! Me poor innocent ould mother!" sez he. "Och, ye murdherin' scoundhril ye, that has murdher in yer heart, murdher on yer face, an'—worse nor all—murdher on yer villainous hands!"

"Aisy, aisy, avic," sez Donal, sez he, "surely ye're not by any mains displaised with me, are ye?" sez he.

"Displaised with ye?" sez the masther, sez he, black in the face—"Is it displaised with ye? I'm not more displaised," sez he, "with the Ould Fella below, himself, sez he, "than I am with ye, ye villain ye!" sez he.

"Thank ye for that," sez Donal, sez he, dancin' with delight. "Down on yer knees," sez he, "till I get them handsome pair o' lugs off ye. You took off my poor brother Myles's lugs, an' I swore I'd be revenged on ye; so ye see I kept me oath," sez he.

So, there the ould masther had nothin' for it but go down on his two knees till Donal got the wool-shears an' clipped the two lugs bare off o' him; an' then gettin' his wages an' his fifty poun' over an' above, he tied up his kit in his red handkerchief, slung his handkerchief on the point of his stick, put his stick over his shouldher, an', whistlin' "The Girl I Left Behind Me," started to home an' to Myles; an' there he foun' Myles an' the farm just as he left them; an' he then with his money bought a naybourin' bit o' lan' that lay into his own, an' himself an' Myles lived the rest o' their lives in full an' plinty, as happy as the day was long. An' that's the end o' MYLES McGARRY AN' DONAL McGARRY.

Nanny and Conn

NANNY AND CONN

ONCE on a time there was a woman and her man named Nanny and Conn, and they lived together quiet and agreeable, in peace, comfort and contentment for eighteen years, when one day, Conn coming from the potato field to get a bit of brakwust, he found my brave Nanny sitting in the chimney corner whillilew-ing and pillillew-ing, crying the very eyes out of her head. When Conn came in she put her apron to her eyes and fell to it like a man to a day's work. "Och, Conn, Conn! Conn darling!" says she. "Why Nanny ahasky," says Conn, says he, "what's the matter with you?" "Och, Conn, Conn, darling!" says she, "but it's me has the sore heart this morning, thinking how it's now eighteen years again' Patrickmas since we were made man and wife, and yet Providence hasn't sent me a son to be a comfort to me now in my old age! Och, Conn, Conn darling!" says she, "but it's the sore pity of me this morning! Ochon! Ochon!" "Well, by my boots," says Conn, says he, "but this beats me entirely; such foolishness I never saw; and I hope," says he, "that I'll see no more of it—for if I did, Nanny," says he, "I couldn't live in the house with you, if you were a princess," and with that Conn turns on his heels and away out he goes to his work again, brakwustless, and whistling, "Father Jack Walsh." My brave Conn wrought away hard at his spade till he said to himself it was a fair dinner time, and then, sticking the spade in the ridge, he starts, whistling, for the house again, wondering to himself all the time if Nanny had done crying yet for her son. But, what would you have of it, when Conn puts his foot on the threshel there was Nanny on one side and a neighbour woman on the other; their two knees met across the fire, with no sign of pot or pan on it, or any thing else that a hungry man would be expecting, and the both of them—och, och, och!— keening and ochoning, one louder nor another, that you'd think the roof would fly off with

itself away off the house, and hard to tell which
of the two of them was the worst.   Conn gave
a sigh and sat down on a creepy stool in the
draught of the door, with his chin on his fists
and his elbows on his knees, and he looking
wonderingly from the one to the other. At
last, when he let them get a wee bit out of
breath, he found his opportunity, and says he,
that way quiet and easy like, "Ma'am," says he,
"haven't ye done with your foolish crying yet
because ye didn't get a son?" says he. "Och,
no, Conn, Conn, Conn darling!" says she,
"that's not what we're crying about now at all,"
says she; "but—och! och! och! ochon!
Sheelah dear! Sheelah dear! Conn asthore!
Conn asthore!—it's something worse! it's
something worse!"   "Well, troth," says Conn,
relieved, "I'm glad to know it's worse. What
is it Nanny, ahasky?" says he. "Why, you
see," says Nanny, "och, och! ye see, it was
Sheelah here, good woman, that come into me
in the morning to know what I was crying
about, and ochon! ochon! just as I was de-
scribing it to her doesn't the marly hen come
stepping in of the door there and fly up on the

roost there, and just as she gets on the roost
doesn't—och! och! ochon! Conn, Conn,
machree! I can't tell it to ye! Ochon, ochon!
As the hen lit on the roost doesn't the roost, bad
cess take it this morning, and the Lord pardon
me for cursing, doesn't the roost ochone, Conn,
Conn! how can I tell it to ye?—doesn't the big
roost come tumbling down, and och, Conn,
ochon! if I had a had the son I was crying for
all the morning the poor child's cradle would
have been maybe in that very spot that the
roost came down on, and the poor innocent
craythur asleep in it, an'—och, Conn, Conn,
darling! there the crathur would have been
killed as dead as a sthone. Och, Conn, Conn,
Conn! Conn, ochone! What's this to do at
all at all? Sheelah *a mhilis!* Sheelah *a mhilis!*
what's this to do?"   And there the two of them
set up the keen again, wringing their hands and
rocking back and forward across the fire. Conn
looked on dumbfounded for a minute, and then
jumping up off the creepy and standing in the
middle of the floor, "Well," says he, "that
bangs Banagher! Such two foolish idiots I
never saw in my life! And by this and by that,"

says he, "if I don't start out this minute, and
I'll never dirty a spade in the ground again, nor
neither of ye will never see my face more till
after I have met three foolisher people than
yous.   After I have met them I'll come home;
but if I don't meet them I'll never come back—
and that's the most likely.   Good-bye to yous,
and God be with yous!"   So spitting on his
stick, he stepped out and travelled away before
him.   He travelled on, and on, and on, till he
come to a cabin, where there was the dirtiest
and wrinkledest and wizenedest old woman you
ever saw, sitting on the roadside before it, and
she trying to sing a love song with a cracked
voice; but she was dressed out with ribbons
that had all the colours of the rainbow.   "God
save ye, ma'am," says Conn.   "God save yerself, kindly," says she; "did ye see ever a king
coming along that road?"   "A what?" says
Conn.   "A king," says the old hag.   "The king
of Ireland," says she, "is now travelling over
the land to pick out the beautifullest girl he can
get to be his wife, and I'm sitting here waiting
till he'll pass, not knowing but what he'd take a
notion of myself.   For ye must know," says she,

"that I was told I was the most beautifullest girl in the three parishes." "When was that?" says Conn, "and who told it to you?" "It was three and sixty years ago," says she, "and the lame beggarman told it to me." "And how long, my good woman, have you been sitting there?" "Seven weeks, exactly, again' the morrow night," says she. "Well, ma'am," says Conn, "I'm the king of Ireland travelling in disguise, and I have now travelled over the whole of my dominions, and I saw many rare beauties, every one of them nicer than the other, but I never saw them I'd put before yerself. It fails me to describe," says he, "the beauty of them silver locks of yours, and them lovely eyes, and your figure and face is beyond compare; the like of your grace I never saw except in a born queen, while as for your complexion, it's like couldn't be found in Ireland again," and there he was telling no lie sure enough. The old hag was all overcome with delight over this. She curtseyed herself down to the ground, and she then threw her skinny arms around Conn's neck and said she was his for evermore. "And now," says she, "wouldn't you like to have some

nice sweet kisses?" For she couldn't get at
Conn's mouth, for he was striving to keep it
as far away from her as he could. "Well, I
don't know," says Conn. "You see the truth
of it is, I've been so accustomed to kissing plain,
ornery looking girls since I set on my journey
—that's plain and ornery when put in compari-
son with your great beauty—I have been so accustomed kissing this sort of girls that I would
be timorous. The sweetest of your kisses,"
says Conn, "might turn my head intirely, and
leave me a raving man for the rest of my
life." "Oh, don't be afraid of that," says she,
"you know you must accustom yourself to mine
anyhow, and one wee one will do ye no harm."
"All right then," says Conn, "let it be a wee
one." And then he held his cheek to her, and
she gave him such a rousing smack as was
echoed up on the hills and sent the wild goats
running helter-skelter over the rocks thinking
someone was shooting at them. "Now ma'am,"
says Conn, says he, "I'm a bit hungry, seeing
meat didn't cross my mouth for the last ten
hours, and I would feel obliged if you'd take me
in and make me a bit of something, for fasting

doesn't agree with a king." "Ah my poor
dear," says she, "it's dead with the hunger you
must be entirely. Come in, *a mhic,* and ye're
welcome to the best my poor house can afford."
So she took him in, and killed her fattest lamb,
and put on a blazing big fire of fir and bog-oak,
and roasted the lamb whole, and set it and a jar
of whiskey before Conn. And my brave Conn
ate like a man who had been fasting, not ten
hours, but ten days, and he drunk like a man
that hadn't drunk since he was weaned,
and then he got up, and brushing down
the crumbs off himself said he was going away
straight back to his palace now to get on a
daicent suit of clothes, and come back with a
bishop and a rajimint of soldiers to marry her.
She was delighted, and she wanted to kiss Conn
going away, but Conn staggered with all the
whiskey he had in him, and "No, no, ma'am,"
says he, "don't ye see that first kiss is in my
head yet." So off he started, himself and his
stick, and says he to himself as he went along,
"Well, Nanny," says he, "there's one foolisher
body in the world than you anyhow, but still
I much misdoubt me if I can get another."

Conn travelled on, and on, and on, till he come
to a house where he found a man having his son
helping him to get under a mule and lift it up.
"God save yez, and good luck to the work,"
says Conn. "God save ye kindly," says the
man back again to him, "and thank ye."
"Could I be of any sarvice to ye?" says Conn.
"If I can ye have only to say it." "Thank ye,
kindly," says the man back again to him, "ye
can." "May I ax what do ye want to do,"
says Conn. "Why," says the man, "it's in regards of them fine long bunches of grass ye see
growing   across   the   roof   of   the   house;
it's a sin, sure, to see them going to loss, and I
want to put up the mule till he eats it." "And,"
says Conn, says he, "could ye find no more convaynient way of letting the mule eat the grass
than that?" "I could not," says the man.
"What do ye think," says Conn, says he, "if I
could point out a way that would make your
mule benefit from the grass without any trouble
to you." "Well," says the man, says he, "I
would think you would be a mighty great
genius entirely; and it would be mortal obli-
gating to me if you could." "What will you

give me, and I will?" says Conn.   "Why," says
the man, "it would be of very great use to
me entirely, and save me all the trouble in the
world; for, at least half a dozen times in the
year, every year, I have to do this, and I have
killed five of my sons at it already, and there's
the sixth and the last, and he'll soon go too;
and I'll be dead myself next with the weight of
that mule lifting him, and holding him up till he
eats the grass.   I'll give ye the mule and the
slide-car," says he, "if ye take it, and tell me an
easier plan."   "It's a bargain," says Conn.   And
then and there he told him to go up on the
house himself and cut the grass, and carry it
down, and give it to the mule.   "By the hokey,"
says the man, says he, "but you're right."   Then
Conn took the mule and the man and his son
hooked him into the slide-car for him, and into
the slide-car he got, and started off.   "Well,
Nanny," says Conn to himself, as he drove
along—"Well, Nanny," says he to himself,
"there's two foolisher people in the world than
you anyhow, but I misdoubt me much if I'll be
able to find a third."   So he drove on, and on,
and on, till he come to a wee cabin on the road-

side after night, and pulling up the mule he
went in, and found no one but an old woman in
the house, and she was so busy down on her
knees blowing the fire that she didn't see Conn
coming in. So down he sat on a seat till she
would be done. "Well, musha, on ye for a
fire," says she, "that ye can't light; I must put
a bit of tallow into ye." So getting up to get
the tallow she sees Conn seated on the chair.
"The Lord protect me," says she, frightened,
"where did you come from?" "From Heaven,"
says Conn. "What, from Heaven?" says she
—"and did you see my Manis up there?" "Yes,
I did, ma'am, surely," says he. "I'll warrant
ye, he's as contentious as ever?" says she.
"Troth, and he is," says Conn, "there isn't a
door in it he hasn't in smithereens." "See that
now," says she, "looking for whiskey, I suppose?" "The very thing," says Conn; "how
did ye know." "Ah, poor Manis," says she,
was always fond of the wee dhrap. I suppose I
will have to send him up some," says she; "Is
there any allowed in?" "Oh, sartinly, sartinly,"
says Conn, "we must allow it in for him, or he
won't leave a sound boord about the whole es-

tablishment he won't smash." "Oh, every
stick and stave," says she; "that's him. I have
just got a wee five gallon here," says she; "do
you think you could manage it up?" "As right
as the mail, ma'am," says Conn; "I have a mule
and a slide-car down with me." "Oh, then, if
ye have," says she, "maybe ye could fetch him
some other little things, too." "With every
pleasure, ma'am," says Conn. "Does Manis
complain of the cold?" says she. "He's just par-
ishing, ma'am," says Conn. "Oh, that's just
Manis for ye," says she; "he was never done
complaining of the cold. Don't ye think hadn't
ye better take him up his overcoat?" "I think
it would be no harm," says Conn. "Is he as
fond of butter as ever?" says she. "He couldn't
live without it, ma'am," says Conn. "Oh, that's
just him—that's just Manis on the sod," says
she; "ye had better take him up that little fir-
kin." "Surely, ma'am," says Conn. "He used
to be very fond of a rasher of bacon," says she.
"It's the very last thing he mentioned to me not
to forget," says Conn. "He's shouting," says
he, "for a rasher and eggs yonder every morning he rises; but the sorra saize the like of

either is to be found in that country." "Poor
man," says she, "that place doesn't agree with
him at all, at all. There, just take up that side of
a pig with you, and here's a couple of dozen of
eggs, too. I'm troubling you too much, good
man," says she, "or I'd be after asking ye to
take a few other wee things." "Don't mention
the trouble at all, ma'am," says Conn; "I assure ye it's only a pleasure to me. As far as
the mule can draw don't spare him, and after
that, pile on to myself," says he. "Well I must
say," says she, stirring herself about the house
and getting together a lot of wee needcessities,
eatables and drinkables and clothes, "I must
say," says she, "you're a mighty obliging man,"
and she commenced piling the things on the
mule till his back was bending down with the
load. "Now," says she, "I think that should
keep Manis's mouth shut for a month of Sun-
days, anyhow. God speed ye," says she to Conn,
"and thanky, and remember me to Manis."
"Thank yourself, good woman," says Conn,
"and the grace of God be about ye. Manis
won't forget ye easy. I'll warrant ye, and he'll
be surely thankful for these things—when he

gets them." So off my brave Conn starts, now in the direction of his home; and he travelled on, and on, and on, whistling and singing, and eating and drinking and going on, and on, and on, till at length when he was coming near home he finds the thiraw* coming behind him, and looking back on the top of a hill he sees the old woman he met at first, and the man he took the mule from, and the last woman he met, all hurry-skurrying behind him with sticks and staves. So he saw they had found out he was tricking them, and were coming after him to take his life. Conn drew the mule and cart into a thick wood, where he hid them; and then turning his coat he commenced cutting scollops. It wasn't many minutes till the hunt was up with him. "My good man," said they, "did you see a man with a mule and cart passing this way a couple of minutes ago?" "I did," says Conn; "a daicent-looking man with a brown coat." "Oh that's him," says they, "but his looks belies him; he isn't as daicent as he is daicent-looking. So signs on it ye had nothing to do with him or ye'd have another story to

---

* Hubbub.

tell.   Tell us what way he went till we take his
life."   "Oh," says Conn, "yez are too late for
that now, for just as he was passing by here—
do ye see that black cloud off there to the nor'-
aist?"   "We do, we do," says they; "what
about that?"   "Why that same cloud," says
Conn, says he, "just as he was passing by here,
that very same cloud came down and carried
himself, the mule and cart right away up to
heaven before my eyes," says Conn.   "See that
now," says they; and they threw down their
sticks, and turned and went away home again.
Then Conn got out his mule and his load, and
started afresh for home, and it's Nanny was delighted to see him, and maybe, too, it's him
wasn't delighted to see Nanny, and he unpacked
his load and gave Nanny as much as would feed
the two of them for twelve months to come.
"And now," says he, "Nanny, I'm back content
and willing to live with you for the remainder
of my days, for I met three such fools that you
would be a wise woman compared with them—
foolish and all as ye are."   And Nanny and
Conn lived a happy life ever afther; and Conn

was never tired of telling that no matter how foolish anyone was there was far foolisher to be met in the world, and them was the truest words ever he omitted.

The Apprentice Thief

"Now Billy Brogan," says the king says he, "what is your son Jack going to turn his hands to?"

THE APPRENTICE THIEF

IT was a lee long time ago when ould Ireland was happy and contented, with lavin's and lashin's—plenty to ait and little to do; and we had our own kings—half-a-dozen of them in every county—and our own Parlymint, and we had mines of all sorts and descriptions, both coal and copper and silver and goold—and, more betoken, the guineas was as common as tenpennies; and the farmers had fields of wheat that it was a day's journey to walk over, and the smell of them was a'most enough to satisfy a hungry man, if the like could be

found in the kingdom—but that would be onpossible, barrin' on a fast day, when (the ould
sinners that they were!) they used to schame it
by goin' out and sniftherin' up the smell of the
wheat, and fillin' themselves (the villains!) that
way, till their fren's would a'most have to
swecl some of them (the rascals) with
ropes, for feared they'd bust; and the blight or
the rot was nivir known on the praties, and they
had tatties that big (the Cups, they called
them) that I heerd me gran'father   say
that he heered his gran'father   say   that
he heerd his great gran'father (I   wish
him rest!) tellin' him, that in the harvest time they often scooped wan   of
them out, and put to *say* in it to fish for mack-
erel—and more betoken, the *say* in them days
swarmed with every description of fish that
ever put a fin in wather, and the fishermen never
used hook or net, but just baled the fishes into
their boats with an ould bucket. Well, how-
andivir, it was in them glor'us days of full and
plenty that Billy Brogan lived as a sort of a
cotthar to the King of Ballyshanny, and Billy
had one son, Jack, that turned out to be very

handy like with his fingers when he wanted anything that didn't belong to him. Well, that fared well till Jack grew up to be a stout, strappin', able lump of a *garsun,* when the king comes to ould Billy, his father, to make complaints on Jack, seein' that he wasn't leaving a movable thing about his castle or grounds but he was hoising off wid him.

"Now, Billy Brogan," says the king, says he, "what is your son Jack going to turn his hands to?"

"Why, yer highness," says Billy, that way, back to him, "throgs, I think he'll turn his hand to anything you laive in his way."

"Och! I know that," says the king, says he, "to my own cost; but I mean to say it's near time you were thinkin' of givin' him a thrade, for the short and the long of it is, that I won't have him about my house or place, longer. I caught him," says he, "only last night thrying to carry off the best mare I have in my stables, Light-o'-foot, and that, you know, is high thrayson; and ye know that the lightest punishment for high thrayson is to be burned, beheaded and hung. But I'll pardon him on con-

ditions that you put him to a thrade at wanst,
and that at the end of three years he'll be so
parfect at the thrade that I can't puzzle him in
any three things I'll put afore him to do; but if
there's any one of them he can't do, he'll have
to suffer his fate for high thrayson."

"Why, yer kingship," says Billy, "the tarms
is mortial hard, stillandiver we'll have to do our
best, and sure the best can do no more. But
what thrade will I 'prentice him to?"

"As for that," says the king, says he,
"plaise yourself, only mind my conditions."

"Well," says Billy, says he, in a brown study
that way, "I think the only thrade that ever I
could make an honest thradesman of him at,
would be a thief, for I think it's the only one
he has the inclinations for."

"Plaise yerself, Billy," says the king back to
him again, "only mind my conditions."

To make a long story short, Billy thramped
off and found Jack, and tould him what the
king of the castle was afther saying.

"Well, father," says Jack, says he, "what
can't be cured must be indured, so you'd betther
be up betimes in the mornin', an' come along

with me till we meet some daicent thief that's masther of his thrade that you'll 'prentice me to, for between ourselves I was long *swithcrin'* to go an' larn the thrade properly anyhow, for though they say that a self-made man is the best, still in this back'ard place one has to work under a great many disadvantages in the up-hill part of the business, so that there's often I would have given my one eye for a couple of good hints from a purficient in the thrade."

No sooner said than done. Jack and his father took the road early next mornin', and a weary travel they had of it that day through a strange country till tor'st night they come to an inn where there was entertainment for man and baste—and for boys too—and they put up there that night, and slept sound I can tell ye, and, moreover, when Billy payed the landlord the damage next mornin', doesn't my brave Jack stale twicet as much back again out of the till before he left. Well they started that morning again and travelled on, and on, of a hot summer's day, when tor'st evening who did they meet but the mastherman thief of all that counthry, and there and then Billy bound over

Jack to him for three years; and he gave Jack his blissin' and told him make the most of his opportunities, and to always keep before his eyes the fear of what he'd meet with from the King of Ballyshanny when he'd come back if he wasn't masther of his trade. Jack promised faithfully that it wouldn't be his fault or he'd know the ins and the outs of the business so far as the ould buck that he was 'prenticed to could put him. Billy then set out for home again, and there was nothing more heerd of me brave Jack till the three years was up.

They weren't long in passing, and on the day afther the end of the three years Jack comes steppin' into his father's house; and Billy, I can tell you, was delighted to see him. He hardly knew him, for he had grown to be as fine and able lookin' a man as you'd meet in the longest day in summer.

"Jack," says his father, says he, throwin' his arms about him, "have ye larned yer thrade?"

"I hope I have, father," says he.

"Jack, *ahaskey*," says the father, "you know what the king has promised if ye're not able to do the three things he puts afore ye?"

"Yes, father," says Jack; "and I'll do my best to do them, and, as yourself says, sure the best can do no more."

Well, that evening the father took Jack up to the castle, and when the king come out he told him that this was Jack come home again afther sarvin' his 'prenticeship, and he had the thrade back with him.

"Why, Jack," says the king, "it's welcome ye are, in troth—*ccud mile failte romhat*— and it's fresh and bloomin' ye're lookin'—what speed did ye come at yer thrade?"

"Why, thank ye kindly, yer highness," says Jack, "I can't complain at all; I think I done very fairly for my time—at laist, that was my masther's opinion, and he's not the worst judge;" for, ye see, Jack was modest and didn't care for puffin' and blowin' about himself.

"Well, it's well for ye, Jack," says the king back to him, "for the three thrials I'll put afore ye will be *no miss,* I assure ye."

"Well, yer kingship," says Jack, "I'll feel honoured to do what I can for ye. Would yer highness be plaised to let me know the first, for it's as well to get the onpleasant business over at wanst?"

"The first thing, Jack, you'll have to do," says the king, "is this: To-morrow morning I'll send out a plough and two horses to plough the tattie field at the back of the hill, and I'll send two men with them, armed to the teeth; and you'll have to stale the two horses out of the plough unknownst to the men, and if ye let to-morrow night fall on ye without having the horses stolen you'll undhergo the punishment for high thrayson—you'll be burned, beheaded and hung; and this time to-morrow I hope to be feasting my eyes on your head stuck on the porch of that gate there. Do you think will ye be able to succeed, Jack?" says he, laughing hearty.

"Why, yer highness," says Jack, "sure I'll do my best, and the best can do no more."

Jack and his father went home; the father very downhearted entirely, seein' that there didn't seem to be any chance for poor Jack at all; and he thought he'd see him burned, beheaded, and hung before his eyes the next night.

Jack didn't say much, but went to bed and
slept sound. He was up with the lark next
mornin', and away out through the fields. He
searched the meadows till he come on a hare
asleep, and catching it he broke one of its legs,
and fetched it home with him. The king sent
out the two horses according to his promise to
plough the tattie field, and he sent with them
two men armed to the teeth, who had sthrict
ordhers that Jack Brogan would attempt to
stale the horses out of the plough that day, but
they weren't to allow him on the paril of their
lives, but were to shoot him if he thried; and
if they allowed him to stale the horses, they
would be hung to the first bush themselves.
Well, of course, they had their eyes about them,
and ploughed, and ploughed away till evening, and no sign of Jack; so they agreed that
Jack had too much wit to run the risk of gettin'
shot, that he had given up the thing in despair,
and had gone and dhrownded himself. With
that they sees a hare with a broken leg coming
over the ditch, and away limpin' across the field
before them. Whirroo! both of them throws
down their guns and swords and afther that

hare for bare life. They didn't go far till they caught it, but when they come back the horses was gone, as clane as if they had nivir been there, and Jack was half roads to the castle with them. He met the king at the gate and handed him over his horses.

"Well, Jack," said the king—and I can tell you he opened his eyes wide when he sees Jack marchin' up to him with the horses—"well, Jack," says he, "ye done that cliverly, but them rascals have been too slack with ye, and I'll take ye in hands myself now. The second thing ye'll have to do—and it's no miss—is to steal the sheet that will be undher myself and the queen when we are sleeping to-morrow night. I'll keep my hand on a loaded gun all night, and the first man enthers my room I'll shoot him dead, and if ye don't succeed in stalin' it, ye know what'll happen ye. What do you think of that, Jack?"

"Well," says Jack, "I'll do my best, and sure ye know the best can do no more."

Then the king was off to ordher out his sojers to hang the two men, and away went Jack home, and you may be sure his father was proud to see him back safe, but when Jack tould him the second thrial, he got down-hearted again, and said he'd surely lose his boy this time.

Jack said nothin', but went to his bed and slept sound that night again; and the next night he went to the graveyard and dug up a fresh corp about the same age as himself, and taking it home he dhressed it in a shoot of his own clothes, and started for the castle in the middle of the night, and gettin' undher the king's bedroom window, he hoisted up the corp, and at the same time threw gravel again the panes.

"What's that?" says the king, jumping up in his bed; and seeing the head at the window he fired, and Jack, with that, let the corp fall.

"Ha, ha," says the king, "I was too able for ye, Jack, my boy; ye're done for at length, and it's yer desarvin'. Now, queen," says he to her ladyship, "I'll have to run out and bury this corp."

Jack waited till he saw the king safe away with the corp, and then he climbed in of the window.

"You weren't long away, king," says her ladyship from the bed.

"Oh," says Jack, purtendin' the king's voice, "I kem back for the sheet to wrap up the corp in an' carry him to the graveyard."

And sure enough, she hands it to him to wrap round the corp, and me brave Jack steps out of the window and away with him.

It wasn't long afther till the king come in with his teeth chattherin', and steps into bed.

"Where's the sheet?" he cried, jumpin' up as soon as he missed it.

"Why, ye *amadan*," says the queen, "didn't ye come back and say you wanted it to wrap up the corp and carry it to the graveyard."

"Oh, Jack—Jack," says the king, lying back in his bed again, "you have thricked me wanst more! But, plaise Providence, that will be the last time."

Next day Jack come to the castle with the sheet rowled up an' ondher his arm, and presented it to the king.

"Well, Jack," says the king, smilin', "ye done me again, but the third time, ye mind, is the charm. To-morrow night I'll sleep with all my

clothes, as well as my shoot of mail, on me, and
you're to steal this inside shirt (showing it to
him) that has my name written on the inside
of the breast of it, ye persave, off my back, and
leave another shirt on me in its place, and I'll
have a loaded gun in every hand all night, and
there'll be a senthry at every window in my
house, and two at every door, and my bedroom will be filled with sodgers; and if ye don't
succeed, ye know what'll happen ye. Eh, what
do you think of that, Jack?"

"Why," says Jack, says he, "sure I'll do my
best, and the best, ye know, can do no more."

Now Jack's father was jumpin' out of his
skin with delight when he found that Jack stole
the sheet, but when Jack come home this night,
an' tould his father that he had to steal the inside shirt, with the king's name on the inside
of the breast, off the king's back, and leave another in its place unknownst to him, while he
slept with all his clothes as well as a shoot of
mail on him, and a loaded gun in every hand,
and with a senthry at every window, and two
at every door, and the room full of sodgers, faix
Jack's father's heart gave way again entirely,

and he said that Jack was as good as lost to him now, anyhow.

Jack said nothing but went to bed and slept sounder now than ever he did, and getting up betimes in the mornin' he went to a tailyer and got him to make a shirt of the same description, and of the very same cloth as the king's inside shirt; and he got the tailyer to prent something in the inside of the breast of it—but what it was we'll not say now. In the middle of the night he rowled up the shirt, and buttoning it up inside his coat, he stharted for the castle. When the senthries seen him comin', they ups with their guns to shoot him, when he shouted out not to mind, for that he was comin' to give himself up, seein' that it was no use in him endayvourin' to do what was onpossible to be done. So, they got round him, and takin' him into the castle, they fetched him to the king's bedroom, where they wakened the king, and told him that Jack had give in at last and couldn't do it.

"Why, Jack," said the king, laughin' hearty, "I knew I would be one too many for ye. Ordher up the hangman at once till we get through with this business."

"Oh, aisy, aisy, if ye plase," said Jack, "sure this was nothin' but a joke of me. I have the shirt already stolen off yer back, and another in its place."

The king swore this was onpossible, and the sojers till a man swore the same, but the king, knowin' Jack was so able, thought it betther not to shout till he was out of the wood; so he pulled off him till he reached the shirt.

"There it is yet, Jack, ye see," says he.

"Is that it?" says Jack. "Is yer name in it?"

"To be sure it is," says the king, readin' it.

"Show me," says Jack; and turnin' round to the light to read the name, purtindin', he slips it undher his coat in the winkin' of a midge's eye, and whips out the other shirt. "Ay, sure enough," says Jack, handin' back *his own*, "that's it all right. So I suppose ye may as well get up the hangman and let us finish off the business at wanst.

"Sartinly, Jack," says the king, gettin' him-self into the shirt and clothes again, "sartinly; delays is dangerous."

But, lo and behould you! when the hangman was got and everything was prepared, the king asked Jack if he had anything to say before h'ed die.

"Why, yes, yer highness," says Jack, "I have a thriflin' wee word to say."

"An' what is it?" says the king. "Out with it, man, and don't be backward about it."

"Why," says Jack, pullin' out the king's shirt from undher his coat, "it's only this—there's yer shirt stolen off yer back, although ye slept in yer clothes and a shoot of mail, and with a senthry at ivery window, and two at ivery door, and yer bedroom filled with sojers, and I have left another shirt on yer back."

The king looked at the shirt and read his name on it, and, turnin' nine colours at wanst, he peeled off him again, and takin' off his inside shirt he read on the inside of the breast of it:—

"Sould again, ould brick !
This is my third thrick—
The shirt taken off yer back
By
    MASTHER-THIEF JACK."

The king was thundher-struck, and no wondher! He ups and he says at wanst, just as soon as he got his senses gathered:—

"Jack," says he, "you must lave my dominions, for I'm not sure but ye might stale the
very teeth out of my head, if ye only took the
notion. I'm sorry, indeed, Jack, but go ye
must. At the same time I'll threat ye daicent
—ye'll have as much gold with ye as yer pockets
can hould."

"Thank ye for nothin'," says Jack back to
him, "for I could have that if yer highness was
to put it undher all the locks in the kingdom.
But I have one requist to ask ye afore I go."

"Name it, Jack," says the king.

"Will ye see that me ould father nivir wants
for anything while he lives?"

"Troth, I will that, Jack, for I'll take him up
to the castle to live along with myself; he'll get
aitin' and dhrinkin' of the best; he'll not be
asked to do a hand's turn of work, and he'll be
as happy as the day is long."

Jack thanked the king hearty, and set out on
his thravels. He went back to the country he
was 'prenticed in, and as his ould masther had
just died, Jack was appointed Masther-man-
thief of that whole counthry, and lived happy
and well ivir afther.

Manis the Besom Man

" It's a half-crown, by the toss o' war!"

MANIS THE BESOM MAN

ONCE on a time when pigs was swine, long,
long ago, there was a man named Manis who
supported himself and his ould disabled mother
by making besoms out of the long heather on
the lonely moor where they lived. One day,
when Manis was driving a very sorry old in-
stitution of a horse—that you could count every
bone in his body through his skin—to the town,
with a load of besoms for sale, he begun to
ruminate to himself on the bad trade this same
besom-making was becoming, entirely, that he
could hardly keep body and sowl sticking together himself, let alone support his mother

and an old horse, that would soon die on his hands anyway; and then he'd be in a fix, for he couldn't scrape as much money together as would buy a new straddle, let alone a new horse. And, as for selling this one, it's what he'd have to pay a man to take him off his hands, let alone get money for him. But it's a bad disaise that can't be cured somehow, Manis said to himself—so he began to consider how he could sell his rickle of a pony to advantage. Manis had about as clever a head as ever was set on ignorant shoulders—and right well he knew this—and he was not long finding a way out of the pickle. When he went to the town and disposed of his besoms, and got the money for them, he put the money into shilling pieces, half-crown pieces, and one half-sovereign, and inquiring for the grandest hotel, he put his horse into the stable, and stuck the gold half-sovereign and all the other pieces into the holes in its hide—for the poor baste's skin had holes enough to hide away a fortune in, goodness knows!—slipping them just what you'd know in under the skin, and then he went into the hotel, and ordered the best of everything,

eating and drinking for himself, and as for the
horse, he told them not to spare the corn and
bran mashes on him, for he was going to put
him into training for a great race. Manis got
all he called for, and the horse, too, got everything of the best, and that all fared well till it
came to the paying of the bill, which reached
a big figure entirely. When the bill was put before him, Manis said he would call again and
pay it; that he had no ready cash about him
now, and all that; but the waiters raised the
divil of a ruction, and sent for the owner of the
hotel himself, who happened to be Mayor over
the town; and they pointed out Manis to him,
and told him the whole story, and the Mayor
said that if Manis didn't take and pay the
money on that instant moment, he would send
for the soldiers and have him hung by coort-
martial at once.

"Well, well," sez Manis, sez he, "but this is a
nice how-do-ye-do, that a gintleman can't be
trusted for a few shillings, only this way. Sweet
good luck to you and your house," sez he to the
Mayor. "I never yet in all my travels met with
such ondaicent people. Though I have a shabby

coat on me atself," sez Manis, "don't judge me
by that, for that's my notion, and it's the way
I choose to go. And look ye here now, Misther
Mayor," sez he, "I could not only pay for
my own dinner, but I could invite every mother's sowl in this town—good, bad, and ondiffer-
ent, big, wee, and middling—here, and give
them their dinners and pay for them, and buy
you out of house and home then, and make a
present of the whole consarn to your waiter
there the next minute, and live as ondependent
as a prence still after," sez Manis. "But if you
must be paid for your hungry bit of a dinner
that wouldn't break a man's fast on a Good Fri-
day, ye must. I left my purse behind me at
home, and I didn't just want to abuse my poor
baste now, seeing he's afther a long journey;
but to stop your throat I'll do anything, so here
goes." And with that Manis plants his hat on
his head and away out to the stables, with the
Mayor and all the waiters after him to see what
he was up to at all, at all.

Manis led out the pony to the yard, and telling the crowd to stand off him, he got the pony
by the head with one hand, and with a stick in

the other he struck the horse's ribs just beside
the place he hid the half-sovereign, and the
horse flung up as well as he was able—bekase
for six years afore he never had the spirit to
fling till he got the feed of corn and bran—
and out jumps the goold half-sovereign, and
rolls just right to the Mayor's feet. The Mayor
looked down at it bewildered.

"Will ye kindly," sez Manis, sez he, in an
offhand sort of way to the Mayor, "will yer
Mayorship kindly pick up that coin and tell me
how much it is?"

The Mayor picked it up, and he looked at
it, and he turned it over and looked at
the other side, and then jingled it on the
ground, and next bit it with his teeth.

"Well, by all that's infarnal," sez he, "but
it's a good shining goold half-sovereign," sez
he, "with the King's head on it."

"Humph!" sez Manis, sez he, "is that all?
That's not enough then, we must try again."

So Manis whacked the horse again, and
again, and again; and the horse flung up again,
and again, and again; and the coins come
jumping out, rolling among the waiters, and

them picking them up and shouting out every time how much they were. When Manis got enough to pay the bill,—

"Now," sez he, "when I have my hand on him, I may as well take the price of a box of matches and a bit of tobacco out of him," and he flogged out another couple of half-crowns, the Mayor and the waiters looking on with their mouths open and rubbing their eyes every now and then to see whether it was asleep or awake they were. When Manis had finished, and had all the pieces flogged out of him except a couple, he yoked him into the cart as if he was going to start.

"I say, my good man," sez the Mayor, when he got his breath with him—"I say, my good man," sez he, "would you sell that horse?"

"Is it sell him?" sez Manis, sez he. "Not by no means."

"I would be content to give you a good penny for him," sez the Mayor; "just as a cur'osity to show my friends, you know."

"You'll have to get some other cur'osity for your friends this time, then," sez Manis. "This would be a rare cur'osity, entirely."

"I wouldn't refuse you fifty pounds down in cold cash for him," sez the Mayor.

"Faix, I suppose you would not," sez Manis, tartly.

"I wouldn't refuse you a hundred pounds down for him, now that I think of it," sez the Mayor.

"Think again," sez Manis.

"Oh, but I considher that a big penny," sez the Mayor.

"And wouldn't you considher five hundred, bigger?" sez Manis.

"Oh, I couldn't think of that, my good man," sez the Mayor.

"Very well and good, then," replied Manis. "When every one sticks to his own, no man's wronged. Good morning and good luck," sez he, pretending to go and to drive off.

"Hold on ye," sez the Mayor, running forward and catching the reins. Is it very expensive, his keep? Have you to feed him on anything special to get them coins out of him?"

"Yes, sartintly," sez Manis, "his keep is a very expensive item entirely, and if you're not purpared to give him his fill of good oat, corn, and bran, there's no use in you throwing away your hard-earned money purchasing him from me. I like to be honest with you, so good morning again."

"Hold on you! Hold on, you!" sez the Mayor, pulling the reins with all his might, for Manis was making wonderful big quivers with the reins and the whip as if he wanted to get away whither or no, and that he was no way consarned to make sale.

"Hold on, you!" sez the Mayor. "One of you run in there," sez he to the waiters, "and fetch me out five-hundred pounds you'll get rolled up in the foot of an old stocking in the bottom corner of my trunk, and the others of you take this horse out of the cart and put him into the stable," sez he.

So the waiter soon come running back with the foot of an old stocking, and the Lord Mayor counted five hundred goold sovereigns out of it down into Manis's hand, and Manis and him parted, Manis going whistling home with a light heart.

The Mayor had the pony locked up in a stable by itself, up to the eyes in corn and bran,

and he double-locked it, putting the key into his
own pocket, and then went round the town telling all his gentlemen friends of his good fortune, and inviting them all to come at twelve
o'clock the next day till they would have the
pleasure of seeing him flogging a hundhred
pound or so out of the horse. Sure enough, at
twelve o'clock the next day, all his gentlemen
friends were gathered in the hotel yard, and the
Lord Mayor come out and opened the stable
door, and ordered one of his men in to lead out
the horse. He was provided with a nice little
tough cane himself, that he had bought at eigh-
teenpence in a little shop next doore, specially
for the occasion, and he ordered his man to lead
the horse into the middle of the yard, and then
he went round clearing a circle about the horse,
putting his gentlemen friends back with the
cane, as he said the little coins would likely be
rolling among them, and would maybe get lost.

"Now, John," says he to the man who was
holding the horse, "keep a good tight grip on
the reins, and don't let him burst away. I'll not
keep you long, for I'll only take a few hundhred
pounds or so out of him the day, just to let these

gentlemen friends of mine see the thing. Hold
hard, now," sez he, and he drew the cane a
sharp slap on the poor baste's ribs.

Up flung the horse, and out jumped a coin,
and rolled into the crowd.

The Lord Mayor crossed his arms, and axed
some of the crowd to lift it and tell him what
was it.

They lifted and examined it, as if it was one
of the seven wonders of the world, and they bit
it, and scratched it, and jingled it, an sez
they,—

"It's a good, bright shilling, with the king's
head on it."

"Humph!" sez the Lord Mayor, a wee bit
taken back, "is that all? I expected a bit of
goold, but the goold's to come yet. Hold hard
again, John!" sez he, and he come down another sharp rap on the horse's ribs. Up flung
the horse, and out jumps another coin. "Kindly
tell me," sez he, crossing his arms, and looking
on indifferently—"kindly tell me," sez he, "how
much is that?"

The crowd took it up again, and scratched it,

and rubbed it, and jingled it, an bit it, and sez
they,—

"It's a half-crown, by the toss o' war!"

"Well, middling, middling," says he, "we're
getting towards the goold now. Hold hard
again, John! Look out, gentlemen, for I'm
guessing this will be a half-sovereign, or a sov-
ereign, and it might get lost." And with that
he comes down another rap on the baste's ribs,
but lo and behold you, though the horse flung
ever so high, the sorra take the coin or coin
come out.

The Lord Mayor looked round him, and then
looked up in the air to see if the coin went up
that way, and forgot to come down; but seeing
no sign of it there, he turned to John, and sez
he,—

"What way did that coin go, John?"

"Faith," sez John, sez he, "you put me a puzzle. Ax me another."

"There's some mistake," says the Lord
Mayor, squaring himself out, and folding up
his sleeves. "I'm afeard I didn't strike hard
enough that time; but it will not be my fault
this time or I will." So down he comes such

a polthogue on the poor brute's bones as made
it's inside sound like a drum, and up higher
than ever the baste flung its heels, and the
Lord Mayor and John, and all the crowd stood
back to watch for the coin, but good luck to
their wit! if they were watching from that time
till this the dickens receive the coin or coin
would they see.

"Right enough," sez the Lord Mayor, sez he,
"it's as plain as a pike staff that there must be
some mistake here. Don't you think isn't there
some mistake, John?"

"Faix," sez John, "I would be very strongly
of the opinion that there is."

"John," sez the Lord Mayor, sez he, "I think
we're not holding his head the right way. It
strikes me that the owner of him held his head
north when he was flogging the money out of
him. What do you think if we hold his head
north?"

"Anything at all you plaise," sez John, "I'm
paid to obey orders."

"All right then, John, just move his head
round that way a little. That's it. That will
do," sez the Lord Mayor. "Now hold hard,

John, and keep a sharp eye out for the coin,"
sez he, spitting on the stick and winding it
round his head, and fetching it down, oh, melia
murdher! that you'd think it wouldn't leave a
bone in the poor baste's body it wouldn't knock
into stirabout.   And then up flung the horse,
and the Mayor jumped back, and they
all jumped back, and then the Mayor
held out his hand and said, "Whisht!
Whisht!" an set up his ears to hear where the
coin would fall; but, movrone, ne'er a coin or
coin was to be heard. The first thing the Mayor
heard was a bit of a titter of a laugh, and then
another and another, till the titter went round
all his gintlemen friends. With that he got
black in the face, to find he had made such a
fool of himself, and to the flogging of the horse
he falls again, determined to have it out of him
if there was a coin at all in him. And
he flogged him high up and low down,
and all around, whacking and striking,
and puffing, and cursing, and the baste
flinging and leaping, and neighing, and
whinnying, till at length ye a'most wouldn't see
the poor animal for blood and foam. And his

gintlemen friends round about had to interfare at last, and drag him away from the horse by brute force, and threaten to give him in charge to the soldiers if he didn't stop murdering the creature, and the horse was dragged off and the Lord Mayor was dragged in, and the whole town laughed for nine days after till they laughed the Lord Mayor clean out of his office. And as for Manis, the rascal, he give up the besom-making trade, as well he might, and he lived an ondependent private jintleman, himself and his mother, for the rest of their days, on the intherest of his money.

Jack and the King Who was a Gentleman

JACK AND THE KING WHO WAS A GENTLEMAN

It is much to be regretted that the Bummadier was not a millionaire; for in that case, at the Bocht money would run like the rain at Lammas. Of course, with a steady and assured income of two pounds five shillings and sixpence per quarter, he was rich enough to be generous—but, alas, not rich enough to be lavish.

There was no other employer of labour at the Bocht to whom the youngsters would give their services with the alacrity they ever showed when the Bummadier had a cart of fir to take in, or rushes to bear home from the Bottoms, to thatch his cabin. And, awaiting their promised pennies, they, in course of time, got to know Pay-day, and to long for it with all the greedy eagerness of the thirstiest old pensioner in the land.

But, in consideration of Pay-day being still
far in the future, Corney was frequently im-
portuned by his mercenaries to acknowledge
their drafts, and pay interest thereon, in the
shape of a good exciting story of the King's-
and-Queen's age.   Which demands, that he
might stave off a run on the bank, the Bummadier was fain to concede.   For the Widow's
Pat, these tales had a thrilling interest, and on
the occasion of one, seated in his usual *siostog*
in the corner, he followed it with such breath-
less excitement as held not even the youngsters
themselves.

Well, childre: wanst upon a time, when pigs
was swine, there was a poor widdy woman
lived all alone with her wan son Jack in a wee
hut of a house, that on a dark night ye might
aisily walk over it by mistake, not knowin' at
all, at all, it was there, barrin' ye'd happen to
strike yer toe again' it.   An' Jack an' his mother
lived for lee an' long, as happy as hard times
would allow them, in this wee hut of a house,
Jack sthrivin' to 'arn a little support for them
both by workin' out, an' doin' wee turns back

an' forrid to the neighbours. But there was one winter, an' times come to look black enough for them—nothin' to do, an' less to ate, an' clothe themselves as best they might; an' the winther wore on, gettin' harder an' harder, till at length when Jack got up out of his bed on a mornin', an' axed his mother to make ready the drop of stirabout for their little brakwus as usual, "Musha, Jack, *a mhic,*" says his mother, says she, "the male-chist—thanks be to the Lord!— is as empty as Paddy Ruadh's donkey that used to ate his brakwus at supper-time. It stood out long an' well, but it's empty at last, Jack, an' no sign of how we're goin' to get it filled again —only we trust in the good Lord that niver yet disarted the widow and the orphan—He'll not see us wantin', Jack."

"The Lord helps them that help themselves, mother," says Jack back again to her.

"Thrue for ye, Jack," says she, "but I don't see how we're goin' to help ourselves."

"He's a mortial dead mule out an' out that hasn't a kick in him," says Jack. "An', mother, with the help of Providence—not comparin' the Christian to the brute baste—I have a kick

in me yet; if you thought ye could only manage
to sthrive along the best way you could for a
week, or maybe two weeks, till I get back again
off a little journey I'd like to undhertake."

"An' may I make bould to ax, Jack," says
his mother to him, "where would ye be afther
makin' the little journey to?"

"You may that, then, Mother," says Jack.
"It's this: You know the King of Munsther is
a great jintleman entirely. It's put on him, he's
so jintlemanly, that he was niver yet known to
make use of a wrong or disrespectable word.
An' he prides himself on it so much that he has
sent word over all the known airth that he'll
give his beautiful daughter—the loveliest picthur in all Munsther, an' maybe in all Irelan',
if we'd say it—an' her weight in goold, to any
man that in three trials will make him
use the unrespectful word, an' say, 'Ye're
a liar!' But every man that tries him, an' fails,
loses his head. All sorts and descriptions of
people, from prences an' peers down to bagmen
an' beggars, have come from all parts of the
known world to thry for the great prize, an' all
of them up to this has failed, an' by consequence

lost their heads. But, mother dear," says Jack, "where's the use in a head to a man if he can't get mail for it to ate? So I'm goin' to thry me fortune, only axin' your blissin' an' God's blissin' to help me on the way."

"Why, Jack, a *thaisge*," says his mother, "it's a dangersome task; but as you remark, where's the good of the head to ye when ye can't get mail to put in it? So, I give ye my blissin', an' night, noon, an' mornin' I'll be prayin' for ye to prosper."

An' Jack set out, with his heart as light as his stomach, an' his pocket as light as them both together; but a man 'ill not travel far in ould Irelan' (thanks be to God!) on the bare-footed stomach—as we'll call it—or it'll be his own fault if he does; an' Jack didn't want for plenty of first-class aitin' an' dhrinkin' lashin's an' laivin's, and pressin' him to more. An' in this way he thravelled away afore him for five long days till he come to the King of Munsther's castle. And when he was comed there he rattled on the gate, an' out come the king.

"Well, me man," says the king, "what might be your business here?"

"I'm come here, your Kingship," says Jack, mighty polite, an' pullin' his forelock, be raison his poor ould mother had always insthructed him in the heighth of good breedin'—"I'm come here, your R'yal Highness," says Jack, "to thry for yer daughter."

"Hum!" says the king. "Me good young man," says he, "don't ye think it a poor thing to lose yer head?"

"If I lose it," says Jack, "sure one consolation 'ill be that I'll lose it in a glorious cause."

An' who do ye think would be listenin' to this same deludherin' speech of Jack's, from over the wall, but the king's beautiful daughter herself. She took an eyeful out of Jack, an' right well plaised she was with his appearance, for,—

"Father," says she at once, "hasn't the boy as good a right to get a chance as another? What's his head to you? Let the boy in," says she.

An' sure enough, without another word, the King took Jack within the gates, an' handin' him over to the sarvints, tould him to be well looked afther an' cared for till mornin'.

Next mornin' the King took Jack with him an' fetched him out into the yard. "Now then, Jack," says he, "we're goin' to begin. "We'll drop into the stables here, an' I'll give you your first chance."

So he took Jack into the stables an' showed him some wondherful big horses, the likes of which poor Jack never saw afore, an' everyone of which was the heighth of the side wall of the castle an' could step over the castle walls, which were twenty-five feet high, without strainin' themselves.

"Them's purty big horses, Jack," says the King. "I don't suppose ever ye saw as big or as wondherful as them in yer life."

"Oh, they're purty big indeed," says Jack, takin' it as cool as if there was nothin' whatsomever astonishin' to him about them. "They're purty big indeed," says Jack, *for this counthry.* But at home with us in Donegal we'd only count them little nags, shootable for the young ladies to dhrive in pony-carriages."

"What!" says the King, "do ye mane to tell me ye have seen bigger in Donegal?"

"Bigger!" says Jack. "Phew! Blood alive,

yer Kingship, I seen horses in my father's stable that could step over your horses without
thrippin'. My father owned one big horse—the
greatest, I believe, in the world again."

"What was he like?" says the King.

"Well, yer Highness," says Jack, "it's quite
beyond me to tell ye what he was like. But I
know when we wanted to mount it could only
be done by means of a step-laddher, with nine
hundred and ninety steps to it, every step a mile
high, an' you had to jump seven mile off the
topmost step to get on his back. He ate nine ton
of turnips, nine ton of oats, an' nine ton of hay,
in the day an' it took ninety-nine men in the day-
time, an' ninety-nine more in the night-time,
carrying his feeds to him; an' when he wanted
a drink, the ninety-nine men had to lead him to
a lough that was nine mile long, nine mile
broad, an' nine mile deep, an' he used to drink
it dry every time," says Jack, an' then he looked
at the King, expectin' he'd surely have to make
a liar of him for that.

But the King only smiled at Jack, an' says
he, "Jack, that was a wonderful horse entirely,
an' no mistake."

Then he took Jack with him out into the garden for his second trial, an' showed him a bee-
skep, the size of the biggest rick of hay ever
Jack had seen; an' every bee in the skep was
the size of a thrush, an' the queeny bee as big
as a jackdaw.

"Jack," says the King, says he, "isn't them
wondherful bees? I'll warrant ye, ye never saw
anything like them?"

"Oh, they're middlin'—middlin' fairish,"
says Jack—*"for this counthry.* But they're
nothin' at all to the bees we have in Donegal.
If one of our bees was flying across the fields,"
says Jack, "and one of your bees happened to
come in its way, an' fall into our bee's eye, our
bee would fly to the skep, an' ax another bee to
take the mote out of his eye."

"Do you tell me so, Jack?" says the King.
"You must have great monsthers of bees."

"Monsthers," says Jack. "Ah, yer Highness, monsthers is no name for some of them.
I remimber," says Jack, says he, "a mighty
great breed of bees me father owned. They
were that big that when my father's new castle
was a-buildin' (in the steddin' of the old one

which he consaived to be too small for a man of his mains), and when the workmen closed in the roof, it was found there was a bee inside, an' the hall door not bein' wide enough, they had to toss the side wall to let it out. Then the queeny bee—ah! she was a wondherful baste entirely!" says Jack. "Whenever she went out to take the air she used to overturn all the ditches and hedges in the country; the wind of her wings tossed houses and castles; she used to swallow whole flower gardens; an' one day she flew against a ridge of mountains nineteen thousand feet high and knocked a piece out from top to bottom, an' it's called Barnesmore Gap to this day. This queeny bee was a great trouble an' annoyance to my father, seein' all the harm she done the naybours round about; and once she took it in her head to fly over to England, an' she created such mischief an' disolation there that the King of Englan' wrote over to my father if he didn't come immaidiately an' take home his queeny bee that was wrackin' an' ruinin' all afore her he'd come over himself at the head of all his army and wipe my father off

the face of the airth. So my father ordhered me
to mount our wondherful big horse that I tould
ye about, an' that could go nineteen mile at
every step, an' go over to Englan' an' bring
home our queeny bee. An' I mounted the horse
an' started, an' when I come as far as the sea
I had to cross to get over to Englan', I put the
horse's two fore feet into my hat, an' in that
way he thrashed the sea dry all the way across
an' landed me safely. When I come to the King
of Englan' he had to supply me with nine hundred and ninety-nine thousand men an' ninety-
nine thousand mile of chains an' ropes to catch
the queeny bee an' bind her. It took us nine
years to catch her, nine more to tie her, an' nine
years and nine millions of men to drag her
home, an' the King of Englan' was a beggar
afther from that day till the day of his death.
Now what do ye think of that bee?" says Jack,
thinkin' he had the King this time sure enough.

But the King was a cuter one than Jack took
him for, an' he only smiled again, an' says he,—

"Well, Jack, that was a wondherful great
queeny bee entirely."

Next, for poor Jack's third an' last chance,

the King took him to show him a wondherful
field of beans he had, with every bean-stalk
fifteen feet high an' every bean the size of a
goose's egg.

"Well, Jack," says the King, says he, "I'll
engage ye never saw more wondherful bean-
stalks than them?"

"Is it them?" says Jack. "Arrah, man, yer
Kingship," says he, "they may be very good—
for this counthry; but sure we'd throw them out
of the ground for useless afther-shoots in
Donegal. I mind one bean-stalk in partickler,
that my father had for a show an' a cur'osity,
that he used to show as a great wondher entirely to sthrangers. It stood on ninety-nine
acres of ground, it was nine hundred mile
high, an' every leaf covered nine acres. It fed
nine thousand horses, nine thousand mules, an'
nine thousand jackasses for nineteen years.
He used to send nine thousand harvestmen up
the stalk in spring to cut and gather off the soft
branches at the top. They used to cut these off
when they'd reach up as far as them (which
was always in the harvest time), an' throw
them down, an' nine hundred and ninety-nine

horses an' carts were kept busy for nine months carting the stuff away. Then the harvestmen always reached down to the foot of the stalk at Christmas again."

"Faix, Jack," says the King, "it was a wondherful bean-stalk, that, entirely."

"You might say that," says Jack, trying to make the most of it, for he was now on his last leg. "You might say that," says he. "Why, I mind one year I went up the stalk with the harvestmen, an' when I was nine thousand mile up, doesn't I miss my foot, and down I come. I fell feet foremost, and sunk up to my chin in a whinstone rock that was at the foot. There I was in a quandhary—but I was not long ruminatin' till I hauled out my knife, an' cut off my head, an' sent it home to look for help. I watched after it, as it went away, an' lo an' behould ye, afore it had gone half a mile I saw a fox set on it, and begin to worry it. 'By this an' by that,' says I to meself, 'but this is too bad!'—an' I jumped out an' away as hard as I could run, to the assistance of my head. An' when I come up, I lifted my foot, an' give the fox three kicks, an' knocked three kings out of him—every one of them a nicer an' a better jintleman than you."

"Ye're a liar, an' a rascally liar," says the King.

"More power to ye!" says Jack, givin' three buck leaps clean into the air, "an' it's proud I am to get you to confess it; for I have won yer daughter."

Right enough the King had to give up to Jack the daughter—an' be the same token, from the first time she clapped her two eyes on Jack she wasn't the girl to gainsay him—an' her weight in goold. An' they were both of them marrid, an' had such a weddin' as surpassed all the weddin's ever was heerd tell of afore or since in that country or in this. An' Jack lost no time in sendin' for his poor ould mother, an' neither herself nor Jack ever after knew what it was to be in want. An' may you an' I never know that same naither.

The Giant of the Band Beggars' Hall

THE GIANT OF THE BAND
BEGGARS' HALL

ONCE upon a time when there were plenty of Kings and Queens in Ireland—it's many of them often we heard of, but few of them ever we seen, except in dhrawin's and picthurs—there was a King and a Queen, and they had one son called Jack. Now, this Jack, when he grew up, was a fine, strong, strapping, able fellow, and he was very fond of fishing. There was one river in particular, alive with trout and fishes of all descriptions, that Jack would never be tired fishing in, but at length the trouts and other fishes in this river begun to get so old-fashioned for him that when they'd find him fishing on one side of the river they would all swim to the other side; and then when my poor Jack would take a boat and cross over to the other side after them, back they'd all swim, and be at the opposite side again by

the time he'd have got to the far bank, and
they'd then commence wagging their tails, the
creatures, out of the water at him tauntingly.
Well, it wasn't in human nature to stand that
sort of thing; no more was it in Jack, for Jack,
of course, was only human; and then Jack
would come home in the evening in the very
devil of a temper, and maybe commence kicking the cat out of spite, bekase the trouts
wagged their tails at him. So this, of course,
more or less vexed the King and the Queen,
and they put their heads together and had long
confabs, consulting what they could do to mol-
lify poor Jack; but the short and the long of it
was, they agreed, let it cost what it might, that
a bridge must be built over the river for Jack,
so that he would be across the river and back
before the trouts could have time to get up their
tails and wag them. Well, the very next day
after this conclusion was come to, all the masons in the country were got together and the
bridge built. Early the next morning Jack was
up and out, and swearing that there would be
no more tails wagged at him or he'd know the
reason why. But, lo, and behold you! when he

come to the place where the bridge was put up
the day afore, there wasn't two stones of it
a-top of other; it was tumbled to the ground
and scattered aist and waist, and there didn't
seem to be a trout in the river but was
gathered to the place, and as soon as Jack put in
an appearance ye would think they were wagging their tails for a wager. Jack turned and
went home, and he met the cat on the hall-door
steps, and he hit her a kick that knocked her
clean through the bottom of a new oaken milk-
tub his mother had out on the steps airing.

"Well, Jack," sez the King, "surely the trouts
aren't wagging their tails at you this morning,
now that we have built ye that beautiful new
bridge, that there isn't the like of it in the country again?"

"Aren't they though?" sez Jack, sez he. "Its
a nice show, your bridge is, this morning, if
ye'd be so kind as to go out and look at it, and
see how there isn't the second stone of it together, and it's the trouts that know it—the
sweet sorra," sez he, "seize the little sowls of
the rascals; I never saw them going through
such tantrums; it's what one old boyo of a

trout that I have had my eye on for the last month curled his tail actually round to his nose," sez he, "and winked his eye out at me," sez he.

"Ye don't tell me so, Jack?" sez the King. "Well, well, this is a purty how d'ye do. Well, Jack," sez he, "I suppose there's no use crying over spilt masonry, no more nor spilt milk, and all we can do is call the masons together again, and build it up."

So, called together they were, and the bridge was up again afore night. And my brave Jack was up with the lark in the morning, and down to the river with his rod, but oh, sorra seize the bridge or bridge was there! It was scattered to the four winds; and the trouts, the scoundhrils, they were ten times more provoking then ever, actually standing on their heads with delight. There was no holding of Jack this morning. He came back from the river in the very mischief of a temper, and not meeting with the cat this time—for she found him coming back—he lifted the milk-tub that his mother had got a new bottom in since, and knocked it

clean through the hall-door and the partition
beyond, into the parlour where the King and
the Queen were sitting at breakfast, scattering
the table and the fine spread of pancakes and tea
all over the room.

"Oh, Jack, Jack,"sez the King, sez he, coming rushing out—"Jack, Jack," sez he; "calm
yourself, calm yourself. You have frightened
your poor mother out of a year's growth, and
spoiled her nice pancakes on her."

"Oh, pancakes be rammed!" sez Jack.

"Jack, Jack," sez the King, sez he; "what—
what's the matter this morning? Surely that
old trout hasn't been putting his tail to his nose
this morning again? If he has," sez he, "trust
me but I'll soon have him taught a trick worth
two of that. He must be let know who's master and who's man here, and that he can't treat
the King's son with disrespect."

"Oh," sez Jack, sez he, "I wish you'd just go
down and look at thon bridge of yours this
morning again, maybe ye'd find reason to un-
derstand then, that not the King's son, but the
King himself is treated with disrespect and con-
tempt."

"Jack," sez the King, taken aback, "surely, Jack," sez he, "ye don't mean to insinuate that the bridge is down again?"

"Don't I though?" sez Jack, with a sneer.

"Well," sez the King, shaking his head, and looking at the ground—"well," sez he, "that flogs the divil."

"I'll tell you what it is," sez Jack. "You put up the bridge once more, and leave the rest of it to me; if it comes down again I'll be able to give an account of myself, and I'll make some devil dance to a tune he didn't call for."

"The third time's the charm," sez the King; "and the third time it will go up, Jack. Then I'll leave the rest of it to you."

So, up it went the third time, and that night Jack determined to sit up and watch the bridge. All went well till about close on midnight, when, Jack being nodding asleep on the bridge, he found it shaking. Up he jumps, and down he runs under the bridge to see what was wrong with it, or who was shaking it, and there, och, och! he beheld the greatest giant he ever saw in his life afore.

"Who are you?" sez the Giant, ready to devore Jack.

"I am the King's son, Jack," sez Jack, sez he.

"Well," sez the Giant, "all rights to this river belong to me, and the King should not have built a bridge over it. By right," sez he, "I should take your life now; but I see," sez he, "you're a smart, clean, active-looking boy, and would be sarviceable to me; and as I never yet took unfair advantage of an enemy, it's not worth my while commencing on you," sez the Giant, sez he, "so I'll give you a chance for your life," sez he. Here's a pack of cards, now," sez he, producing a pack, "and I'll play you a fair game. If you win, you'll get your life, and I'll let the bridge remain, but if I win I'll either take your life on the spot or put a condition on you. Do you agree to that?"

"Done," sez Jack, for he thought to himself it would be all the one anyhow, whether he agreed to it or not.

"What game will it be?" sez the Giant.

"Short, and be done with it; we'll make it twenty-five," sez Jack.

"All right," sez the Giant, "cut for deal."

Jack cut and won the deal.   He shuffled and dealt them, turned a five and won three tricks.

"That's sharp for me, Jack," says the Giant, as he shuffled.

Jack got a slashing hand again.   Spades was trumps, and Jack led with the ace, but the big fellow covered with the ace of hearts, raised again with the fingers of trumps, and followed up with the knave, a twinkle in his eye all the time.

Jack threw down his cards.

"Ha, ha! Jack," says the Giant, "too able for ye?   Eh?   No odds though," sez he; "you're not a bad hand at the flats, and have a deal of spunk in you, so I'll give ye a chance for your life yet."

"What's that?" sez Jack.

"It's this," says the Giant.   "Within a year and a day from this you're to find out my castle, where I live when I'm at home: but if you're not able to find it, then I'll have your life, toss this bridge, and leave the highest stone in your father's castle the lowest."

"And who are you?" sez Jack.

Sez the Giant,—

> " I'm the Giant of Band-beggars' Hall,
> The greatest Giant over them all."

"I have never heard of your castle," sez Jack.

"Nor I hope never will," sez the Giant.

"Well, that's to be seen," says Jack.

So the Giant and he parted, and Jack went home—for it was now morning—and told the King and Queen all that had happened. They were greatly vexed entirely, and cursed it for a misfortunate bridge, and tried to persuade Jack to remain at home and not go away on such a wild-goose chase, to the Lord knows where, looking for

> "The Giant of the Band-beggars' Hall,
> The greatest Giant over them all."

But Jack wasn't to be persuaded, and whether or why, he would go, and never rest till he would find him out, or else lose his life. So he spit on his stick, and, taking his father's and mother's blessing, started off that very day. And Jack travelled afore him for months, without ever once stopping, or eating a bite, or sleeping a wink; and at nightfall one day, he came to a great castle on a lonely moor in the

Easthern World, and he went in and saw a
Giant sitting by the fire. When Jack came in,
the Giant got up, and sez he,—

"You're very welcome, Jack, the King of
Ireland's son, for I haven't seen the face of a
Christian for the last three hundred years."

Jack wondered how he knew his name, but
he didn't say anything. The Giant then put
Jack sitting by a roaring fire, and taking a
knife he cut down the quarter of a rat that was
hung in the smoke of the chimney and roasted it
on the coals, and himself and Jack made a hearty
supper of it, and then each of them slept on a
harrow with a goatskin under them and another
over them, and Jack slept hearty and well, for
he was very tired entirely. Next morning he
rose as fresh as a butterfly, and after breakfast-
ing on another quarter of the rat, sez the Giant,
sez he,—

"I didn't ask you, Jack—where were you
going?"

"No more you might," sez Jack; "I might
tell you where I'm coming from, but where I'm
going is more than I knows."

So Jack starts and he tells him the whole story

about him and the Giant of the Band-beggars'
Hall. And then he asked him if he could give
him any tidings of where he lived?

"Well, no," sez the Giant, "I heard of him
only, and that was all. But I'll tell you what
I'll do," sez he. "I have command of a third
of the birds of the air, and it's likely some of
them may know something about him, and if
they do I'll soon find it out for you," sez he.

So with that he blew a whistle, and immediately from all corners of the sky the birds
begun for to gather, and very soon they were
all round the castle, making the sky dark. Then
the Giant put it to them did they know anything
of—

> " The Giant of the Band-beggars' Hall,
>   The greatest Giant over them all,"

or where he lived.

But no, they said they heard tell of him only,
but none of them ever reached where he lived.

"Well," sez the Giant, sez he to Jack, "it's
bad enough. But I'll tell you what," sez
he. "I'll give you a pair of nine-mile boots,
and with them you'll reach an older brother of
mine who lives a long ways off entirely, and he

has command over half the birds of the air, and maybe he could do something for you."

Jack thanked him, and putting on the boots he started away and travelled on, and on, and on, nine mile at every step, till late at night he reached the Giant's older brother's castle away on a very lonely moor, and going in he saw the Giant sitting by the fire. The Giant got up and he says,—

"You're welcome Jack, the King of Ireland's son, for I haven't seen the face of a Christian for six hundred years. You stopped at my brother's house last night," sez he.

"I did," sez Jack, all the time wondering how he knew him, or where he stopped last night, but he said nothing.

Then the Giant put Jack beside the big fire, and cutting down two quarters of a rat that was hung in the smoke of the chimney, he roasted them, and Jack and he ate a quarter a piece, and then they went to bed, everyone of them on a harrow, with a goatskin under them and another over them; and Jack slept well and sound for he was very tired, and got up as fresh as a butterfly in the morning, and when they had eaten a good breakfast of the other half of the rat the Giant asked Jack where was he going.

"Well," sez Jack, sez he, "I might tell you how far I come, but I can't tell you how far I am going," and he ups and he tells this Giant the whole story too.

"Well," sez the Giant, sez he, "it's bad enough, but I'll do all I can to help you. I heard tell of the Giant of the Band-beggars' Hall, and that's all I know about him; but I have command over half the birds of the air, and it's likely some of them may know something about him, and if they do I'll soon find out."

So he took out a little whistle and blew it, and in a minute the sky commenced to darken with great flocks of birds flying from all corners, and they all gathered round the Giant's castle. Then the Giant, he put the question to them, if any of them in their travels had come across the Giant of the Band-beggars' Hall,

"The Giant of Band-beggars' Hall,
The greatest Giant over them all."

But none of them had ever come across him.

They had heard tell of him, they said, but that was all.

"Well, it's bad enough," sez the Giant to Jack, "but there's one other remedy yet. I'll lend you a pair of nine-league boots; and I have a brother lives a day's journey from here, by them, who has command over all the birds of the air, and maybe he'll be able to help you."

So off Jack set in the nine-league boots, and late that night he reached the third Giant's house. When he went in, he saw the Giant sitting by the fire, and he got up and welcomed Jack.

"You're welcome, Jack," sez he, "the King of Ireland's son, for I haven't seen the face of a Christian for the last nine hundred years. You slept at my brother's house last night."

Then he sat Jack down by the fire, and reaching up the chimney he took down a rat that was hanging in the smoke, and roasting it on the fire, himself and Jack made a hearty supper of it. And they went to bed, each of them lying on a harrow, with a goat-skin over them and one under them. And Jack slept well and sound, and got up in the morning as fresh as a butterfly. And after they had made a good breakfast on another rat, sez the Giant, sez he,—

"Jack, may I ask you how far you intend going?"

"Well," sez Jack, sez he, "I may tell you how far I come, but as to how far I'm going it's more nor I could tell."

So he starts and he tells the Giant the whole story, and he then asked him if he could give him any information as to where the Giant of the Band-beggars' Hall lived?

"Well, no," sez the Giant, sez he, "I heard tell of the Giant of the Band-beggars' Hall, but that was all. But I'll tell you what I'll do," sez the Giant. "I have command of all the birds of the air, and I'll call them together to see if they would know anything about him."

So the Giant blew a whistle, and in a minute the sky was darkened by all the birds of the air gathering together from all corners. And when they were all gathered over the castle the Giant put it to them—Did any of them know anything of

" The Giant of the Band-beggars' Hall,
The greatest Giant over them all."

But, lo and behold ye, not one of them knew a thing about him; they had heard tell of him, they said, but none of them ever reached to where he lived.

Poor Jack got into bad heart at this intelligence.

"What will I do now," sez Jack, sez he, to the Giant, "for I'm done now, out and out?"

"I don't know, Jack," sez the Giant. "But hold," sez he, "on second thoughts there's one eagle that isn't here. He flies everywhere over the whole known world, and only comes here to see me once in seven years, and I'm expecting him to-day, for it's just seven years this day since he was with me before. Wait till we see, when he comes, if he has any tidings of him; and if he hasn't I don't know what you'll do."

And sure enough, that very evening they saw the monstrous big eagle—the like of it, for size, Jack never saw before—coming in a thundercloud, darkening the very sky with its wings; and when the Giant saw this, sez he,—

"Now, Jack," sez he, "it will not do to let you be seen by the eagle, for he would eat any human being he would see, especially now, when he is coming home ravenous after his big fly."

So he sewed Jack up in a big leathern bag, and hung him by the side of the chimney. And as soon as the eagle had come, the Giant welcomed him and asked him if there was any news.

"No," sez the eagle very sharp, "where would I get news? I'm dead with hunger," sez he; "and get me something to eat at once. It will be better for me than gossiping news with you."

So the Giant went and fetched in a bullock and twelve lambs; and the eagle fell to at once and ate them, bones and all; and he then put his head into his wings and went asleep at once. And the Giant went to bed, too; and Jack was still in the leathern bag, listening to and watching all that was going on. It was late the next morning when the eagle awoke after his big feed. When he did he called for breakfast, and the Giant fetched him in another bullock and twelve lambs, and he ate these up quickly, bones and all; and when he had finished he stroked down his breast with his beak, and flapped his wings two or three times.

"Now," sez he, "I'm myself again."

"Do ye know," sez the Giant, sez he to him, "do ye know, or have ye met in all your travels, the Giant of the Band-beggars' Hall?"

"What would I know about him?" sez the eagle. Then, sez he, "I was there once, but I'll never go there again, for it's away out of the world entirely."

"Well," sez the Giant, "he was here lately, and he left that bag to be sent to his place, and he is to behead me if I don't get it there."

"Well, I'll not take it," sez the eagle.

"Very well, then," sez the Giant," I suppose I must wait on my fate."

At last, after some time, the eagle sez, sez he,—

"Well, you know, I'm under an obligation to you and your family, and I couldn't refuse you anything; so, I suppose I must take it."

So the Giant took the bag into a room; to sew a burst that was in it, he told the eagle. Then he put in with Jack as much provisions as would last him for a twelve-month. He bid Jack good-bye and wished him God-speed. And Jack heartily thanked him. He then sewed up

the bag again and gave it to the eagle. He
took it up and started away on his flight, and
he flew on, and on, and on, till the days turned
to weeks, and the weeks to months, and poor
Jack thought they would never reach their journey's end. But at length, when they were
nearly a year out—though it seemed to Jack to
be twenty years since they started—Jack found
the eagle slackening in his flight, and coming
down, and down, and down, lower and lower,
till at length they touched ground, and Jack
cut a little hole in the bag to look out of, and
there he saw a castle far greater than all the
castles put together that ever he had seen before, and out of it there comes a great Giant,
and when Jack saw him he didn't know whether
to be glad or sorry, for it was no other nor

"The Giant of the Band-beggars' Hall,
The greatest Giant over them all."

"You're welcome," sez the Giant to the eagle.
"It's so long since you were here I thought I'd
never see your face more."

"It's seldom come the better," sez the eagle;
"you'll never see it again if I have my will.
And, indeed," sez he, "if it wasn't for this bag

I was sent with to you, you wouldn't see me now. There it is," sez the eagle, "and good-bye."

So off he flew, and the Giant said to himself he wondered who would be sending a bag to him, or what was in it. So, taking out a big clasp-knife, he cut open the bag, and out my brave Jack steps, and,—

"How do ye do," sez Jack, sez he, "the Giant of Band-beggars' Hall, the greatest Giant over them all?"

Well, the Giant, when he caught a glimpse of Jack, was staggered and dumbfoundered.

"Well, Jack," sez he, at length, when he come to himself, "ye're a most wonderful fellow. This bangs all ever I knew," sez he. "I surely thought that I had the better of you; but I see you were too clever by half for me. And I'll stand to my contract, for you deserve to have your life spared. And more than that," sez he, "I have a young daughter that I never intended to let marry—for I couldn't think to get a husband for her that would be to my liking, till I fell in with you—but now that I have met you and seen the uncommon clever man you are entirely, you can have her if she takes your fancy, with a heart and a half, and a handsome fortune."

Jack said nothing to this till he would see her, for he had a fancy that no matter what fortune she might have—and he suspected the fortune such a Giant could give with her would be no miss—he could find nicer girls in Ireland. But, och, when he saw the very first sight of her, the beauties of Ireland all flew out of his head, and he was head and ears in love with her at once, for the like of her for pure downright loveliness he never before laid his two eyes on. And when her father asked her what she thought of Jack, she couldn't contain herself, she was that much in love with him. So the thing was settled up at once, for Jack was thinking of his poor father and mother grieving for him at home, and couldn't delay. Then the Giant of the Band-beggars' Hall counted out to Jack, as a fortune with the beauty, a sword that the man who fought with it couldn't be beaten, and a loaf of bread that would never grow less no matter how much was cut off it, and a flask of whisky that would never be emp-

tied no matter how much was drunk from it,
and a purse that would always be full no matter how much was taken out of it.   He then
gave them two wishing-caps that they had only
to put them on their heads and wish to be
any place, and they would be there.   So they
took the Giant's blessing, and putting their caps
on their heads, wished to be at the oldest of the
three brother Giant's house that helped Jack;
and when they come there Jack gave him the
sword, for he said he had no use for it, seeing
there wasn't a man in Ireland he was afraid of.
They then put on their caps and wished to be
at the next Giant's; and when they come there,
Jack gave him the loaf, for he said Ireland
never yet knew want.   Then, they put on the
caps again, and wished to be at the first Giant's
house that Jack fell in with, and when they
came there, Jack gave him the flask of whiskey,
for, he said, the rivers in Ireland flowed with it.
He kept the purse for himself, saying that he
could do good with it.   They then put on their
caps, and wished to be home in the King's Castle in Ireland; and home they were at once.
And that was the reception was for them!   And

there was the joy and the rejoicing! And all the
country was asked in to the wedding. And such
a spread of eating and drinking, and carousing,
lasting for nine days, was never known in Ireland afore! But Jack first went on the bridge,
and hooked the trout that put its tail to its nose,
and winked its eye about at him, and he stuck
that trout against the wall with a corker pin
through its body for the nine days the feast
lasted, till it saw all the rejoicement, and wriggled and twisted, and heartily repented having
ever been unrespectful to Jack. From that day
forward Jack fished to his heart's content off
the bridge, and he caught no end of the trouts
for they couldn't trick him any longer, and none
of them ever afterwards wagged their tails out
of the water at Jack, and himself and his beautiful wife lived happy ever after.

www.ingramcontent.com/pod-product-compliance
Lightning Source LLC
Chambersburg PA
CBHW031400270326
41929CB00010BA/1262